Creative
ÉCLAIRS

DISCARDED

Creative ÉCLAIRS

Over **30** fabulous flavours
& easy cake-decorating ideas
for choux pastry creations

RUTH CLEMENS

D&C
David and Charles
www.stitchcraftcreate.co.uk

CONTENTS

ON THE MENU

STRAWBERRIES & CREAM

ORANGE SUNBURST

APPLE PIE

RASPBERRY RIPPLE

ZESTY LIME

TROPICAL FRUIT MEDLEY

LEMON SYLLABUB

SUMMER PUDDING

CLASSIC CHOCOLATE

MANGO & PASSION FRUIT

PEACH MELBA FANTASY

SUGAR & SPICE

RUM & RAISIN

BERRY BURST

NUTTY CRUNCH

INTRODUCTION

WELCOME to *Creative Éclairs*! Choux pastry is often thought of as difficult to make and perfect, but in fact it's the easiest pastry you'll ever make. It's really not that difficult as long as you follow some basic rules – and it's extremely rewarding watching the magic puff that takes place inside the oven. Used to make éclairs, profiteroles and puffs, choux pastry is deliciously light and crisp, requiring only few basic ingredients. Once you've made it, choux is so versatile it can play host to a million different fillings, toppings, shapes and decorations. And it's equally delicious munched straight off the cooling rack!

Beautiful to look at, éclairs are even better shared and eaten. There are recipes in this book to cover all tastes. You'll find all your favourite fillings and toppings as well as a selection of other more creative projects that put choux pastry to good use. Choose your favourite or mix and match.

So whether you fancy rustling up a batch of classic chocolate éclairs for a family treat or attempting the construction of a croquembouche the size of the Eiffel Tower for a dramatic centrepiece, you'll find all the tips, tricks and recipes you need right here. You may even feel inspired to create your own masterpiece!

Ruth x

TOOLS & EQUIPMENT

Baking & filling

Scales

Measuring spoons

Medium saucepan

Wooden spoon/spatula

Baking trays (sheets)

Non-stick baking (parchment)
paper/silicone liners
(bake-o-glide)

Vegetable or sunflower oil spray

Wire cooling rack

Sharp serrated knife

Disposable piping (pastry) bags

Selection of choux piping nozzles
(tips): 18mm (¾in) serrated
open (French type) for éclairs
(Wilton 8B, 6B, 4B); 1.5cm (⅝in)
round open nozzle for puffs

Small piercing nozzle

Selection of filling nozzles
(tips): filler/Bismarck nozzles,
open star piping, round piping

Decorating

Electric hand whisk

Edible gel paste colours

Small disposable piping
(pastry) bags

Sugarcraft cutters – flowers,
blossoms, stars, hearts,
circles, rose petals

Sugarpaste (rolled fondant/
ready-to-roll icing) rolling pin

Ball tool for sugarcraft modelling

Sugarcraft leaf veiners

Edible lustre dusts

Small paintbrushes

Edible rejuvenator fluid or clear
alcohol (such as vodka or gin)

Selection of small piping
nozzles (tips)

HOW TO CHOUX

HOW TO MAKE ÉCLAIRS

Ingredients

75ml (2½fl oz) water

55ml (2fl oz) whole milk

55g (2oz) butter

5ml (1 tsp) vegetable or sunflower oil

¼ tsp salt

1 tsp sugar

100g (3½oz) plain (all-purpose) flour

4 large eggs

Sunflower or vegetable oil spray

Variation

To make a chocolate choux pastry, reduce the plain (all-purpose) flour to 75g (2¾oz) and add 25g (1oz) cocoa powder (unsweetened cocoa)

Equipment

Medium-sized pan

Wooden spoon

Baking sheet

Non-stick baking (parchment) paper/ reusable silicone liners (bake-o-glide)

Disposable piping (pastry) bag

15mm (⅝in) plain round piping nozzle (tip) for profiteroles, or 18mm (¾in) French style serrated nozzle (tip) for éclairs

Makes approximately 12 x 15cm (6in) éclairs, 15 x 12cm (4¾in) éclairs, 18 x 10cm (4in) éclairs

Making Choux Pastry

Method

1. Place the water, milk, butter, oil, salt and sugar in a medium pan. Heat over a medium heat stirring frequently until the butter has melted. Bring to the boil and add the flour.

2. With the pan still on the heat, beat the mixture with a wooden spoon until it comes together into a ball.

3. Turn the heat down to low and continue to mix over the heat for 3 minutes. This helps to reduce any excess moisture and changes the paste from a rough shaggy texture to a much smoother, glossy paste. Remove from the heat and allow to stand for 2 minutes to cool slightly.

4. Add the eggs one at a time, beating the choux well after each addition until all the eggs have been incorporated.

∽ TIP ∽

With each egg addition, the mixture will appear to separate and slide around the pan. However, the choux will suddenly incorporate as you beat, at which point it's ready for the next egg to be added.

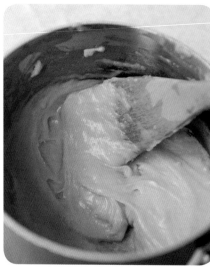

5. Continue to mix until the consistency returns to a smooth, glossy texture before adding the next egg.

6. When all the eggs have been incorporated, the choux pastry will be glossy with a thick, medium-firm texture.

7. Transfer to a bowl and cover with cling film (plastic wrap). Allow to cool fully then refrigerate for at least 1 hour. This makes the choux pastry much easier to pipe neatly.

❧ TIP ☙

Be aware of the consistency of the choux when adding the eggs if making a double or triple batch. You may need less than the full amount of eggs required if not working in single batches.

Piping the Choux

1. Once chilled, transfer the choux pastry to a piping (pastry) bag fitted with an 18mm (¾in) piping nozzle (tip). A serrated pen (French style) nozzle (tip) is ideal for éclairs as it creates ridges in the piped éclairs which allow the dough to expand evenly on baking, avoiding any cracking across the top.

2. Preheat the oven to 160°C (fan)/180°C/350°F/Gas Mark 4. Pipe the choux pastry into éclairs or choux buns of the desired size using an even pressure to keep the width of each éclair the same.

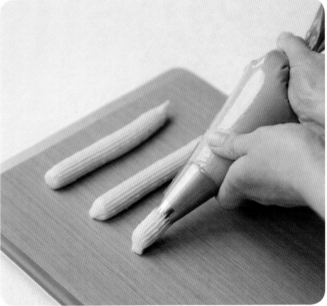

☙ TIP ❧

Choux pastry will only keep for one day in the fridge once prepared. If preferred, it can be frozen straight away in a sealed container and defrosted before use. Alternatively, pipe into long lengths and freeze without wrapping. Remove and cut to length with a sharp serrated knife before storing in a freezer bag for up to 1 month. The choux can also be baked from frozen – simply spray lightly with oil and add an extra 10 minutes to the baking time.

3. Any peaks or misshapen ends can be smoothed with a dampened finger once piped.

4. Spray the éclairs lightly with a vegetable or sunflower oil. This can be bought in ready-filled pump sprays or you can easily fill a spray bottle yourself at home. This light coating prevents the crust from forming on the éclairs too early in the baking process, allows the choux pastry to expand evenly, and helps prevent the top of the finished éclair from cracking. (Fry Light or a cake release oiling spray will have the same effect and work equally well.)

HOW TO MAKE ÉCLAIRS

5. Bake in the oven for: 15cm (6in) éclairs – 50 minutes; 12cm (4¾in) éclairs – 45 minutes; 10cm (4in) éclairs – 40 minutes. See individual projects for specific baking and cooling advice.

✑ TIP ✑

Choux pastry can be piped out and snipped off at the required length with a pair of lightly greased scissors if preferred.

✑ TIP ✑

Piped, chilled choux pastry will hold its shape well without spreading. However, if the choux pastry is still warm, it will flow and flatten, in which case it must be chilled further before piping into the required shape.

FILLING & TOPPING RECIPES

INGREDIENTS

600ml (20fl oz) whole milk

Seeds scraped from 1 vanilla pod,
5ml (1 tsp) vanilla bean paste
or 5ml (1 tsp) vanilla extract

100g (3½oz) caster
(superfine) sugar

4 large egg yolks

50g (1¾oz) cornflour
(cornstarch)

EQUIPMENT

Large jug

Whisk

Medium-sized pan

Cling film (plastic wrap)

Large bowl

Electric hand mixer

Vanilla Crème Patissière

METHOD

1. In a large jug whisk together the egg yolks and caster (superfine) sugar until the mixture is light and foamy. Add the cornflour and whisk again until of an even consistency. Set to one side.

2. Place the milk and vanilla in a medium pan and heat gently until just below boiling point. Whilst whisking the egg mixture continuously, add the warmed vanilla-infused milk a little at a time until both mixtures have been fully worked together.

❧ TIP ❧

Make sure you whisk together the egg yolks as soon as the caster (superfine) sugar is added to them. This will prevent the sugar from pulling the moisture out of the yolks, which could result in 'egg burn', where you would have yellow flecks in your finished crème patissière.

3. Transfer the mixture back to the pan and over a medium heat, whisking continuously, bring to the boil. Continue to cook the crème patissière for 2 minutes until thick and glossy.

4. Remove the pan from the heat and transfer the mixture to a bowl. Contact-cover the top of the crème patissière with cling film (plastic wrap) to prevent a skin from forming, and allow to cool. Refrigerate once cooled.

5. When you are ready to use it, transfer the chilled crème patissière to a large bowl and beat with an electric hand mixer until it is a smooth and even consistency.

VARIATIONS

CHOCOLATE

Omit the vanilla from the milk and prepare as vanilla crème patissière. Before transferring to a bowl to cool, whisk in 15g (½oz) cocoa powder (unsweetened cocoa) and 20g (¾oz) finely grated dark chocolate. Chill and beat fully before using.

MOCHA

Replace the vanilla in the milk with 2 teaspoons of instant coffee. Before transferring the crème patissière to a bowl to cool whisk in 15g (½oz) cocoa powder (unsweetened cocoa) and 20g (¾oz) finely grated dark chocolate. Chill and beat fully before using.

GINGER CHOCOLATE

Omit the vanilla and add 1 ball of finely grated stem ginger to the milk. Allow to infuse for 1 hour before making as for the vanilla crème patissière. Whisk in 15g (½oz) cocoa powder (unsweetened cocoa) and 20g (¾oz) finely grated dark chocolate before cooling. Beat fully before using.

White chocolate

Prepare as the vanilla crème patissière but before transferring to a bowl to cool, whisk in 150g (5½oz) melted white chocolate.

Chocolate orange

Omit the vanilla and add the grated zest of 1 orange to the milk. Before transferring to a bowl to cool, whisk in 45g (3 tbsp) cocoa powder (unsweetened cocoa) and 5ml (1 tsp) orange extract.

Coconut

Replace the milk with 400ml (14fl oz) coconut milk and 200ml (7fl oz) double (heavy) cream. Omit the vanilla and prepare as vanilla crème patissière.

Malted milk

Omit the vanilla from the milk and add 60g (4 tbsp) malted milk drink powder. Prepare as vanilla crème patissière.

Nutty choc

Omit the vanilla from the milk and before transferring to a bowl to cool, whisk in 30g (2 tbsp) cocoa powder (unsweetened cocoa) and 140g (5oz) hazelnut chocolate spread such as Nutella.

Mango & passion fruit

Replace the milk with 600ml (20fl oz) mango and passionfruit smoothie, omitting the vanilla, and prepare as vanilla crème patissière.

Raspberry & cranberry

Replace the milk with 300ml (10fl oz) raspberry-based smoothie and 300ml (10fl oz) cranberry juice. Omit the vanilla and prepare as vanilla crème patissière.

Orange

Replace the milk with 600ml (20fl oz) fresh orange juice (with or without bits). Omit the vanilla and prepare as vanilla crème patissière.

Lime

Replace the vanilla with the zest of 1 lime and add to the milk. When beating the crème patissière just before using, whisk in 30ml (2 tbsp) lime juice.

Tropical

Omit the vanilla and replace with the grated zest of 1 lime, half an orange and half a lemon. Before transferring to a bowl to cool, whisk in 15ml (1 tbsp) coconut liqueur.

∽ TIP ∽

Crème patissière can be made up to one day in advance and kept in the fridge until needed. It does not freeze well as it has a tendency to split.

INGREDIENTS

250ml (9fl oz) double
(heavy) cream

25g (1oz) icing
(confectioners') sugar

5ml (1 tsp) vanilla bean paste
(or the seeds from 1 vanilla pod)

VANILLA CHANTILLY
CREAM QUANTITIES

Double (heavy) cream	Icing (confectioners') sugar	Vanilla bean paste
300ml (10fl oz)	30g (1oz)	5ml (1 tsp)
400ml (14fl oz)	40g (1½oz)	7.5ml (1½ tsp)
500ml (18fl oz)	50g (1¾oz)	10ml (2 tsp)

VANILLA CHANTILLY CREAM

METHOD

1. Place all the ingredients in a large bowl and whisk together with an electric hand whisk until the cream forms soft peaks. Vanilla Chantilly cream can be made a couple of hours in advance and stored in the fridge until needed.

∽ TIP ∽

It is important to only whip the cream very softly at this stage. Spooning, folding in additions, and piping from a bag will work the cream further and you don't want it to become overwhipped.

INGREDIENTS

Dark Chocolate Ganache

150g (5½oz) good quality dark (semisweet) chocolate

75ml (2½fl oz) double (heavy) cream

White Chocolate Ganache

175g (6oz) white chocolate

75ml (2½fl oz) double (heavy) cream

Milk Chocolate Ganache

50g (1¾oz) dark (semisweet) chocolate

125g (4½oz) white chocolate

75ml (2½fl oz) double (heavy) cream

CHOCOLATE GANACHE

METHOD

1. Chop the chocolate into fine pieces and put into a heatproof bowl.

2. Heat the cream in a small pan until just below boiling point. Remove from the heat and pour it over the chopped chocolate.

∽ TIP ∽

The finer the chocolate is chopped before pouring over the hot cream, the faster it will melt. This avoids reheating the ganache to remove any lumps of chocolate and stops the chocolate cream from being overheated, which could cause the ganache to split.

3. Cover the bowl and allow to stand for 3 minutes before stirring to a smooth even glossy ganache. If necessary the mixture can be gently warmed if pieces of unmelted chocolate remain.

4. Allow to cool. Ganache will need to be warmed gently to return it to a liquid state for covering the tops of éclairs.

VARIATION

RASPBERRY CHOCOLATE GANACHE

To make a raspberry version, chop and gently melt 165g (5¾oz) white chocolate either in a bowl over a pan of steaming water or gently in the microwave. Remove from the heat and stir through 60ml (4 tbsp) raspberry purée until evenly combined. Allow to cool. Raspberry ganache needs to be warmed gently to the correct consistency for dipping éclairs before use.

INGREDIENTS

300g (10½oz) white sugarpaste (fondant/ready-to-roll icing)

30ml (2 tbsp) water

EQUIPMENT

Heatproof bowl

Small pan or microwave

Electric hand mixer

METHOD

1. Break the fondant into small pieces and place in heatproof bowl with the water.

2. Heat gently in the microwave in short bursts, or over a pan of steaming water, stirring frequently, until the fondant melts.

∽ TIP ∽

Fondant glaze can be coloured with food gel pastes and easily flavoured with a wide range of extracts. Simply add a small amount of gel paste colour in the required shade to warmed fondant that is ready to be used. Make sure that it is evenly mixed to avoid any streaks before using to coat the tops of éclairs.

3. Mix with an electric mixer until the consistency is smooth and even and no lumps remain. The glaze will begin to set while it cools, so use while it is still warm. It can easily be reheated to pouring consistency if it cools too quickly for use.

✧ TIP ✧

The temptation is to add more water to keep the fondant in a liquid state but if you do this the fondant will not set once the éclairs are coated. Gently warming the fondant before use is the best method.

COFFEE

Dissolve 5g (1 tsp) of instant coffee in 30ml (2 tbsp) hot water before adding to the fondant and heating together.

CHOCOLATE

Dissolve 15g (1 tbsp) of cocoa powder (unsweetened cocoa) in 30ml (2 tbsp) hot water before adding to the fondant and heating together.

Ingredients

2 large cooking apples, peeled, cored and diced into 1cm (½in) cubes

40g (1½oz) caster (superfine) sugar

½ tsp ground cinnamon

¼ tsp ground nutmeg

50ml (2fl oz) water

Other Fillings & Toppings

Apple pie filling

Method

Place the diced apples in a pan with the sugar, cinnamon, nutmeg and water. Heat over a gentle heat for about 5 minutes, stirring frequently, until the apple has softened and the mixture has thickened. Transfer to a bowl and allow to cool.

 TIP

Apple pie filling can easily be made in the microwave. Simply place all the ingredients in a heatproof bowl and microwave on full power for 2 minutes at a time, stirring well, until the apple chunks fall and the mixture thickens.

Ingredients

50ml (2fl oz) double (heavy) cream

35g (1¼oz) caster (superfine) sugar

20g (¾oz) golden (corn) syrup

15g (½oz) demerara sugar

15g (½oz) butter

Caramel glaze

Method

Prepare the caramel glaze. Place the cream, sugars and syrup in a small pan. Heat gently, stirring frequently, until the sugars dissolve fully. Turn up the heat and bring the mixture to the boil without stirring. Allow to simmer for 3 minutes before removing from the heat and adding the diced butter. Stir until the butter has melted and the mixture is smooth and even.

TIP

Caramel glaze can be made in advance and stored in an airtight container until needed. It should be warmed to the correct consistency before dipping the tops of the éclairs.

INGREDIENTS

Zest of 1 lemon and juice of 2 (approx.100ml/3½fl oz)

70g (2½oz) caster (superfine) sugar

450ml (16fl oz) double (heavy) cream

160g (5¾oz) lemon curd

LEMON SYLLABUB FILLING

METHOD

Place the lemon zest, juice and caster (superfine) sugar in a small bowl. Stir together then set aside and leave to soak for 4 hours. Pour the double cream into a large bowl, add the lemon mixture and whisk until the cream forms soft peaks. Gently fold through the lemon curd.

∽ TIP ∽

To get the most juice from lemons, before squeezing heat the lemons whole in a microwave for 15 seconds. Cut in half and squeeze – you will almost double the amount of juice!

INGREDIENTS

1x quantity milk chocolate ganache, warmed

1 x 390g (14oz) jar (drained weight 250g/9oz) black cherries in kirsch or fresh pitted cherries

400ml (14fl oz) softly whipped double (heavy) cream

CHOC CHERRY FILLING

METHOD

Warm the milk chocolate ganache gently to soften. Blitz the drained black cherries in a food processor or using a hand blender, then fold together with the softly whipped cream and ganache.

∽ TIP ∽

Fresh pitted cherries will work just as well in this choc cherry filling if black cherries in kirsch are difficult to get hold of.

FILLING & TOPPING RECIPES

FILLING, DIPPING & SPLITTING

FILLING ÉCLAIRS

1. Pierce the base of the éclair once at each end using a small piping nozzle (tip) (for larger 15cm/6in éclairs, also pierce a hole in the middle of the base).

2. Add the filling to a piping (pastry) bag fitted with a filling tip – these are also known as Bismarck tips or cupcake filler nozzles (tips), such as Wilton 230.

3. Insert the filler nozzle (tip) into the pierced hole at one end and squeeze in the filling gently. Remove the tip and place it into the hole at the opposite end and fill again, just until you see a little movement of the filling at the hole in the opposite end.

4. Clean off any excess filling from the base of the éclair with your fingertip or by swiping it across the lip of a small jug.

✑ TIP ✑

Just cooled choux will take more filling than completely cold ones as there is still some flexibility in them. This allows the éclairs to expand slightly as you fill.

Dipping Éclairs

1. Place the warmed liquid ganache or fondant in a shallow open bowl – big enough to fit the length of the éclair easily.

2. Dip the top of the éclair into the mixture. Then with one end leading and the rest following, moving in an arc to remove it from the bowl and allow the excess to drain from one end.

3. Place each éclair onto a wire rack, glazed-side up to set.

∽ TIP ∽

As fondant sets fairly quickly at room temperature, it is best to add any decorations to each éclair as soon as they have been dipped rather than waiting for the whole batch to be coated.

SPLITTING ÉCLAIRS

1. Open filled éclairs need to be split in two. Using a sharp serrated knife, start at one end and work along the length of the éclair in a sawing-type motion. Work carefully so as not to shatter the crust, keeping the bottoms and tops of the éclair together as a pair while you work so that they match when you come to put them back together.

2. Place the éclair on the work surface and fill the base section, using an open star or plain nozzle, as preferred. Note that split éclairs should contain a firmer filling that will hold its own shape, such as cream-based fillings.

❦ TIP ❦

The insides of larger éclairs and choux shapes may contain webbed choux. If so, after splitting, this can be gently scooped out using a spoon and discarded to make way for more filling.

A LITTLE BIT OF HISTORY...

ÉCLAIRS conjure up the sights and smells of a beautiful Parisian pâtisserie, but where did they originate and what is the history behind this classic and delicious little bake?

Well, they do indeed come from a beautiful Parisian pâtisserie! Some speculate that they were invented in the 19th century by the famous French chef-to-high-society and cookery writer, Antonin Carême. Said to be the first celebrity chef, he worked his way from lowly kitchen boy to internationally renowned chef, cooking culinary masterpieces for the likes of Napoleon and King George IV.

Choux pastry, however, stretches even further back in history to 1540, when Catherine de Medici fled with her entire court when her family were ousted as rulers of Florence. It is widely believed that one of her chefs, Pantarelli, invented a small puff-shaped dessert with vibrant flavours and decorative flourishes – the pâte à popelin was born.

Over the following centuries Pantarelli's recipe evolved into pâte à choux, and when our friend Antonin Carême got his hands on them he made some modifications to the recipe, continuing the evolution into profiteroles and éclairs!

© e-MagineArt.com

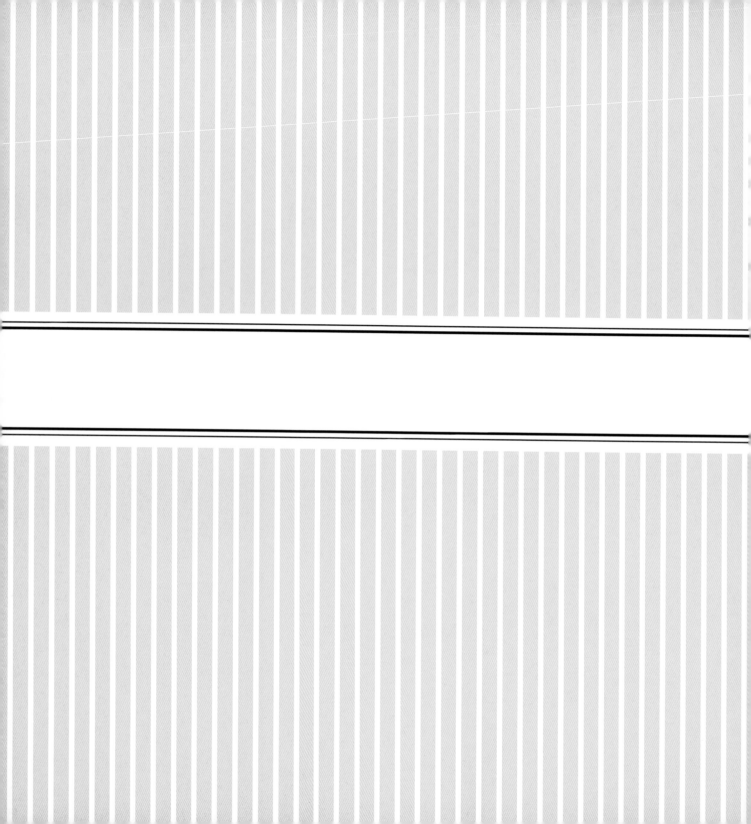

FRUIT FANTASTIQUE

STRAWBERRIES & CREAM

Makes 15 x 12cm
(4¾in) éclairs

INGREDIENTS

1 x quantity choux pastry
(see How to Make Éclairs)

550g (1lb 4oz) strawberries

1 x quantity vanilla Chantilly
cream, made with 500ml
(18fl oz) double (heavy) cream
(see Filling & Topping Recipes)

Icing (confectioners')
sugar, to dust

METHOD

1. Preheat the oven to 160°C
(fan)/180°C/350°F/Gas Mark 4. Fill a
piping (pastry) bag fitted with an 18mm
(¾in) nozzle (tip) with the chilled choux
pastry. Pipe 12cm (4¾in) éclairs onto a
baking sheet lined with non-stick baking
(parchment) paper or a silicone liner
(bake-o-glide). Spray the éclairs lightly
with vegetable or sunflower oil and bake
in the preheated oven for 45 minutes
until golden brown. Transfer to a wire
rack and allow to cool completely.

2. Wash and hull the strawberries
and slice finely.

∾ TIP ∾

When strawberries are not in
season they can be replaced with
other seasonal fruits. Or you could
even use a layer of good-quality
strawberry preserve instead.

ASSEMBLY

1. Split each éclair using a sharp serrated
knife (see Filling, Dipping & Splitting).

2. Place the vanilla Chantilly cream
in a piping (pastry) bag fitted with
an open star nozzle (tip) and pipe the
cream onto the base of each éclair.

3. Top with the sliced strawberries.

4. Position the tops of the éclairs
and dust with a little icing
(confectioners') sugar. Serve.

RASPBERRY RIPPLE

Makes 15 x 12cm
(4¾in) éclairs

INGREDIENTS

1 x quantity choux pastry
(see How to Make Éclairs)

1 x quantity vanilla Chantilly
cream, made with 400ml
(14fl oz) double (heavy) cream
(see Filling & Topping Recipes)

140g (5oz) raspberries, puréed
and sieved to remove seeds

1 x quantity raspberry
chocolate ganache (see Filling
& Topping Recipes)

Decorations

White sugarpaste (rolled
fondant/ready-to-roll icing)

Pink and green edible lustre dusts

50g (1¾oz) icing
(confectioners') sugar

METHOD

1. Preheat the oven to 160°C
(fan)/180°C/350°F/Gas Mark 4. Fill a
piping (pastry) bag fitted with an 18mm
(¾in) nozzle (tip) with the chilled choux
pastry. Pipe 12cm (4¾in) éclairs onto
a baking sheet lined with non-stick
baking (parchment) paper or a silicone
liner (bake-o-glide). Spray the éclairs
lightly with vegetable or sunflower oil
and bake in the oven for 45 minutes
until golden brown. Transfer to a wire
rack and allow to cool completely.

2 Purée the raspberries and sieve to
remove the seeds. Fold gently through
the vanilla Chantilly cream and set aside.

3. Make small rolled roses and
leaves for each éclair using white
sugarpaste (see Sugarcraft Techniques).
Gently dust the roses in pink lustre
dust and the leaves in green.

ASSEMBLY

1. Place the raspberry cream in a piping
(pastry) bag fitted with an open star
nozzle (tip). Split each éclair using
a sharp serrated knife and pipe the
raspberry cream into the base of each
éclair (see Filling, Dipping & Splitting).

2. Warm the raspberry chocolate ganache
gently until of a dipping consistency and
place in an open shallow bowl. Dip the
tops of each éclair in the ganache to coat
and place on top of the cream-filled bases.

3. Mix the icing (confectioners')
sugar with a little water to a fairly
thick consistency and place in a
small piping (pastry) bag. Drizzle in
lines across the raspberry ganache
(see Piping Techniques) and top each
with a rolled rose and leaf. Serve.

LEMON SYLLABUB

Makes 10–12 x
15cm (6in) éclairs

INGREDIENTS

1 x quantity choux pastry
(see How to Make Éclairs)

1 x quantity lemon syllabub filling
(see Filling & Topping Recipes)

1 x quantity pale yellow
fondant glaze (see Filling
& Topping Recipes)

Decorations

White sugarpaste (rolled
fondant/ready-to-roll icing)

Orange edible lustre dust

Rejuvenator fluid or clear alcohol

50g (1¾oz) icing
(confectioners') sugar

Green gel paste food colouring

METHOD

1. Preheat the oven to 160°C
(fan)/180°C/350°F/Gas Mark 4. Fill a piping
(pastry) bag fitted with an 18mm (¾in)
nozzle (tip) with the chilled choux pastry.
Pipe 15cm (6in) éclairs onto a baking sheet
lined with non-stick baking (parchment)
paper or a silicone liner (bake-o-glide).
Spray the éclairs lightly with vegetable or
sunflower oil and bake in the oven for 50
minutes until golden brown. Transfer to a
wire rack and allow to cool completely.

2. Make medium and small blossoms
from white sugarpaste and set aside to
dry (see Sugarcraft Techniques). Mix a
little orange lustre dust with rejuvenator
fluid and use a small paintbrush to paint
a dot in the centre of each blossom.

ASSEMBLY

1. Pierce the base of each éclair
three times, once at either end
and once in the middle.

2. Place lemon syllabub filling in a piping
(pastry) bag fitted with a filling nozzle (tip),
such as a Wilton 230, and use to fill each
éclair (see Filling, Dipping & Splitting).

3. Warm the pale yellow fondant glaze
gently until of a dipping consistency and
place in an open shallow bowl. Dip the
top of each éclair in the fondant to coat.

4. Mix the icing (confectioners')
sugar with a little water to a fairly
thick consistency, colour pale green
and place in a small piping (pastry)
bag. Pipe a scattering of small green
leaves across the tops of the éclairs.

5. Add the white sugarpaste
blossoms, sticking each in position
on the base of a leaf. Serve.

MANGO & PASSION FRUIT

Makes 18 x 10cm
(4in) éclairs

INGREDIENTS

1 x quantity choux pastry
(see How to Make Éclairs)

1 x quantity mango &
passion fruit crème patissière
(see Filling & Topping Recipes)

1 x quantity yellow fondant glaze
(see Filling & Topping Recipes)

Decorations

½ x quantity royal icing
(see Sugarcraft Techniques)

Purple gel paste food colouring

2 tbsp freeze-dried mango

METHOD

1. Preheat the oven to 160°C
(fan)/180°C/350°F/Gas Mark 4. Fill a piping
(pastry) bag fitted with an 18mm (¾in)
nozzle (tip) with the chilled choux pastry.
Pipe 10cm (4in) éclairs onto a baking sheet
lined with non-stick baking (parchment)
paper or a silicone liner (bake-o-glide).
Spray the éclairs lightly with vegetable or
sunflower oil and bake in the oven for 40
minutes until golden brown. Transfer to a
wire rack and allow to cool completely.

2. Prepare a batch of royal icing
and colour it purple. Place in a
small piping (pastry) bag fitted
with a no. 43 nozzle (tip).

ASSEMBLY

1. Whisk the chilled mango & passion
fruit crème patissière with an electric
hand mixer until smooth and place in
a piping (pastry) bag fitted with a filling
nozzle (tip), such as a Wilton 230.

2. Pierce the base of each éclair
once at each end and fill with mango
& passion fruit crème patissière
(see Filling, Dipping & Splitting).

3. Warm the yellow fondant glaze gently
until of a dipping consistency and place
in an open shallow bowl. Dip the top
of each éclair in the fondant to coat.

4. Pipe a snail trail (see Piping
Techniques) of purple royal icing
down the centre of each and scatter
over freeze-dried mango. Serve.

RUM & RAISIN

Makes 18 x 10cm
(4in) éclairs

INGREDIENTS

1 x quantity choux pastry
(see How to Make Éclairs)

1 x quantity vanilla crème
patissière (see Filling &
Topping Recipes)

125g (4½oz) raisins

100ml (3½fl oz) dark rum

1 x quantity pale cream
fondant glaze (see Filling
& Topping Recipes)

Decorations

40g (1½oz) raisins

METHOD

1. Preheat the oven to 160°C
(fan)/180°C/350°F/Gas Mark 4. Fill a piping
(pastry) bag fitted with an 18mm (¾in)
nozzle (tip) with the chilled choux pastry.
Pipe 10cm (4in) éclairs onto a baking sheet
lined with non-stick baking (parchment)
paper or a silicone liner (bake-o-glide).
Spray the éclairs lightly with vegetable or
sunflower oil and bake in the oven for 40
minutes until golden brown. Transfer to a
wire rack and allow to cool completely.

2. Soak 125g (4½oz) raisins in dark rum
for 4 hours (or overnight), then drain
and reserve the liquid. Blitz in a food
processor or with a stick blender until fine.

ASSEMBLY

1. Beat the chilled vanilla crème
patissière together with the blitzed
raisins and 15ml (1 tbsp) of the
reserved rum using an electric hand
mixer. Place in a piping (pastry) bag
fitted with a filling nozzle (tip).

2. Pierce the base of each éclair once at
each end and fill with rum & raisin crème
patissière (see Filling, Dipping & Splitting).

3. Finely dice the remaining raisins.

4. Warm the pale cream fondant glaze
gently until of a dipping consistency
and place in an open shallow bowl.
Dip the top of each éclair in the
fondant to coat and scatter with the
finely chopped raisins. Serve.

ORANGE SUNBURST

Makes 18 x 10cm
(4in) éclairs

INGREDIENTS

1 x quantity choux pastry
(see How to Make Éclairs)

1 x quantity orange crème
patissière (see Filling &
Topping Recipes)

1 x quantity white
fondant glaze (see Filling
& Topping Recipes)

Decorations

Orange edible lustre dust

Rejuvenator fluid or
clear alcohol

METHOD

1. Preheat the oven to 160°C
(fan)/180°C/350°F/Gas Mark 4. Fill a piping
(pastry) bag fitted with an 18mm (¾in)
nozzle (tip) with the chilled choux pastry.
Pipe 10cm (4in) éclairs onto a baking sheet
lined with non-stick baking (parchment)
paper or a silicone liner (bake-o-glide).
Spray the éclairs lightly with vegetable or
sunflower oil and bake in the oven for 40
minutes until golden brown. Transfer to a
wire rack and allow to cool completely.

2. Mix together a little orange lustre dust
with rejuvenator fluid or clear alcohol
to form an orange-coloured paint.

TIP

Paint made with dusts and
rejuvenator fluid or clear alcohol
dries out quickly, so it can't be
made up in advance. Use for
decorating as soon as it is mixed.

ASSEMBLY

1. Beat the chilled orange crème
patissière with an electric hand
mixer until smooth and place in a
piping (pastry) bag fitted with a filling
nozzle (tip) such as a Wilton 230.

2. Pierce the base of each éclair once
at each end and fill with orange crème
patissière (see Filling, Dipping & Splitting).

3. Warm the white fondant glaze gently
until of a dipping consistency and place
in an open shallow bowl. Dip the top
of each éclair in the fondant to coat.

4. Dip a stiff paint brush into the orange
paint and flick the bristles to splatter
orange across the fondant tops. Serve.

ZESTY LIME

Makes 10–12 x 15cm
(6in) éclairs

INGREDIENTS

1 x quantity choux pastry
(see How to Make Éclairs)

1 x quantity lime crème
patissière (see Filling &
Topping Recipes)

1 x quantity white
fondant glaze (see Filling
& Topping Recipes)

Decorations

Lime green sugarpaste (rolled
fondant/ready-to-roll icing)
(see Sugarcraft Techniques)

METHOD

1. Preheat the oven to 160°C
(fan)/180°C/350°F/Gas Mark 4. Fill a piping
(pastry) bag fitted with an 18mm (¾in)
nozzle (tip) with the chilled choux pastry.
Pipe 15cm (6in) éclairs onto a baking sheet
lined with non-stick baking (parchment)
paper or a silicone liner (bake-o-glide).
Spray the éclairs lightly with vegetable or
sunflower oil and bake in the oven for 50
minutes until golden brown. Transfer to a
wire rack and allow to cool completely.

2. Roll out the lime green sugarpaste
thinly and cut out large, medium and
small circles (see Sugarcraft Techniques).
Carefully cut out the centres of half of the
large green circles and set aside to dry.

ASSEMBLY

1. Beat the prepared lime crème
patissière with an electric hand mixer
until smooth and place in a piping
(pastry) bag fitted with a filling nozzle
(tip) such as a Bismarck or Wilton 230.

2. Pierce the base of each éclair
three times, once at each end and once in
the middle. Fill with lime crème patissière
(see Filling, Dipping & Splitting).

3. Warm the white fondant glaze gently
until of a dipping consistency and place
in an open shallow bowl. Dip the top
of each éclair in the fondant to coat
and position a variety of lime green
circles on the top of each. Serve.

TIP

When cutting out the centres, try to lift out the smaller cutter with
the sugarpaste centre still held within it; these can then be gently
eased out and used for decoration, too. If the centre doesn't release
after cutting, it can be gently lifted out with a cocktail stick.

SUMMER PUDDING

Makes 18 x 10cm (4in) éclairs

INGREDIENTS

1 x quantity choux pastry (see How to Make Éclairs)

1 x quantity vanilla crème patissière (see Filling & Topping Recipes)

150ml (5fl oz) softly whipped double (heavy) cream

Summer Fruits

150g (5½oz) raspberries

100g (3½oz) blackberries

50g (1¾oz) blackcurrants

1 tbsp caster (superfine) sugar

METHOD

1. Preheat the oven to 160°C (fan)/180°C/350°F/Gas Mark 4. Fill a piping (pastry) bag fitted with an 18mm (¾in) nozzle (tip) with the chilled choux pastry. Pipe 10cm (4in) éclairs onto a baking sheet lined with non-stick baking (parchment) paper or a silicone liner (bake-o-glide). Spray the éclairs lightly with vegetable or sunflower oil and bake in the oven for 40 minutes until golden brown. Transfer to a wire rack and allow to cool completely.

2. Place the summer fruits and caster (superfine) sugar in a bowl, mix together and mash gently with a fork.

ASSEMBLY

1. Split each éclair with a serrated knife (see Filling, Dipping & Splitting).

2 Beat the chilled vanilla crème patissière with an electric hand mixer until smooth and gently fold in the softly whipped double cream. Place in a piping (pastry) bag fitted with a serrated open nozzle (tip).

3. Divide the summer fruits between the éclairs, spooning the mixture onto the bases.

4. Pipe five to six bulbs of crème patissière mixture along the lengths and replace the tops. Serve.

PEACH MELBA FANTASY

Makes 15 x 12cm
(4¾in) éclairs

INGREDIENTS

1 x quantity choux pastry
(see How to Make Éclairs)

2 peaches, peeled,
halved and stoned

150g (5½oz) raspberries,
puréed and sieved

225g (8oz) mascarpone cheese

2 tbsp icing (confectioners') sugar

300ml (10fl oz) double
(heavy) cream

Decorations

Peach sugarpaste (rolled
fondant/ready-to-roll icing)
(see Sugarcraft Techniques)

100g (3½oz) icing
(confectioners') sugar

Peachy gel food paste
pink colouring

Pink and gold edible lustre dusts

METHOD

1. Preheat the oven to 160°C
(fan)/180°C/350°F/Gas Mark 4. Fill a
piping (pastry) bag fitted with an 18mm
(¾in) nozzle (tip) with the chilled choux
pastry. Pipe 12cm (4¾in) éclairs onto
a baking sheet lined with non-stick
baking (parchment) paper or a silicone
liner (bake-o-glide). Spray the éclairs
lightly with vegetable or sunflower oil
and bake in the oven for 45 minutes
until golden brown. Transfer to a wire
rack and allow to cool completely.

2. Soak the peach halves in the raspberry
purée for 4 hours or overnight. Remove
the peaches from the raspberry purée,
dice and set aside, reserving the purée.

3. Roll out the peach sugarpaste and
cut out fantasy leaf shapes. Using a
veiner, imprint the markings on the
leaves (see Sugarcraft Techniques).
Set aside to dry in the recesses of an
egg box or tray to hold their shape.

ASSEMBLY

1. Whisk together the mascarpone cheese,
icing (confectioners') sugar and cream until
the mixture forms soft peaks. Fold through
the reserved raspberry purée and place the
mascarpone filling in a large piping (pastry)
bag fitted with an open star nozzle (tip)

2. Split each éclair with a sharp
serrated knife and fill each base with
the raspberry mascarpone filling
(see Filling, Dipping & Splitting).

3. Top the cream filling with pieces of
diced peach melba and replace the lids.

4. Mix the icing (confectioners') sugar
with a little water to a thick consistency
and colour it peachy pink. Place in
a small piping (pastry) bag and pipe
two wavy lines of icing over the top of
each éclair (see Piping Techniques).

5. Dust around the edges of the dry
leaves with pink lustre dust and
dust the centres with gold. Add a
fantasy leaf to each and serve.

BERRY BURST

Makes 18 x 10cm
(4in) éclairs

INGREDIENTS

1 x quantity choux pastry
(see How to Make Éclairs)

1 x quantity raspberry
& cranberry crème
patissière (see Filling &
Topping Recipes)

1 x quantity white
fondant glaze (see Filling
& Topping Recipes)

Decorations

Peach and pink sugarpastes
(rolled fondant/
ready-to-roll icing)
(see Sugarcraft Techniques)

METHOD

1. Preheat the oven to 160°C
(fan)/180°C/350°F/Gas Mark 4. Fill a piping
(pastry) bag fitted with an 18mm (¾in)
nozzle (tip) with the chilled choux pastry.
Pipe 10cm (4in) éclairs onto a baking sheet
lined with non-stick baking (parchment)
paper or a silicone liner (bake-o-glide).
Spray the éclairs lightly with vegetable or
sunflower oil and bake in the oven for 40
minutes until golden brown. Transfer to a
wire rack and allow to cool completely.

2. Roll out the peach and pink sugarpastes
thinly and cut out a variety of small
medium and large hearts (see Sugarcraft
Techniques). Set aside to dry.

ASSEMBLY

1. Beat the chilled raspberry & cranberry
crème patissière with an electric hand
mixer until even and add to a piping
(pastry) bag fitted with a filling nozzle
(tip) such as a Bismarck or Wilton 230.

2. Pierce the base of each éclair
once at each end and fill with the
raspberry & cranberry crème patissière
(see Filling, Dipping & Splitting).

3. Warm the white fondant glaze gently
until of a dipping consistency and place
in an open shallow bowl. Dip the top of
each éclair in the fondant to coat and
scatter over the sugarpaste hearts. Serve.

 TIP

These decorations can be made well in advance – once dried they can be
stored in a jar or container (not airtight) and will keep for several weeks.
Any excess left over after decorating can be kept for future use.

APPLE PIE

Makes 12 x 12cm
(4¾in) éclairs

INGREDIENTS

1 x quantity choux pastry
(see How to Make Éclairs)

½ x quantity vanilla crème
patissière (see Filling &
Topping Recipes)

1 x quantity apple pie filling
(see Filling & Topping Recipes)

1 x quantity caramel glaze
(see Filling & Topping Recipes)

Decorations

Small amounts of red, brown
and green sugarpaste (rolled
fondant/ready-to-roll icing)
(see Sugarcraft Techniques)

METHOD

1. Preheat the oven to 160°C
(fan)/180°C/350°F/Gas Mark 4. Fill a
piping (pastry) bag fitted with an 18mm
(¾in) nozzle (tip) and pipe 12cm (4¾in)
éclairs onto a baking sheet lined with
non-stick baking (parchment) paper or
a silicone liner (bake-o-glide). Spray the
éclairs lightly with vegetable or sunflower
oil and bake in a preheated oven for 45
minutes until golden brown. Transfer to a
wire rack and allow to cool completely.

2. Prepare the apple decorations. Roll
balls of red sugarpaste, roughly 1cm
(½in) in diameter. Using a skewer or the
wrong end of a paintbrush poke a hole
into the top of each. Roll a thin sausage
of brown sugarpaste for the stalk and
set it into the hole in the apple. For the
leaf roll a small ball of green sugarpaste,
flatten the ball between your fingertips
and pinch one end to form the sharp
point of the leaf. Score a central vein
down the centre of the leaf and secure
in position on the top of the apple using
a small dab of water. Set to one side.

ASSEMBLY

1. Slice the tops off the éclairs,
dividing them into roughly two thirds
for the base, one third for the top.

2. Beat the chilled vanilla crème patissière
with an electric hand mixer until smooth.
Place in a piping (pastry) bag fitted with
a 1cm (½in) round open nozzle (tip).

3. Fill the base of each éclair with
apple pie filling (see Filling, Dipping
& Splitting) and pipe small bulbs of
vanilla crème patissière on top.

4. Warm the caramel glaze to a
pourable consistency if necessary
and place in a shallow bowl, at least
as wide as the length of the éclairs.

5. Dip the top surface of each éclair
top into the caramel glaze and place
into position on top of each filled
éclair base. Add an apple decoration
to the top of each. Serve.

TROPICAL FRUIT MEDLEY

Makes 10–12 x 15cm
(6in) éclairs

INGREDIENTS

1 x quantity choux pastry
(see How to Make Éclairs)

1 x quantity tropical crème
patissière (see Filling &
Topping Recipes)

60g (2¼oz) fresh
pineapple, sliced

70g (2½oz) fresh kiwi, sliced

50g (2¼oz) fresh mango, sliced

1 x quantity orange fondant glaze
(see Filling & Topping Recipes)

Decorations

Yellow and lime green
sugarpaste (rolled fondant/
ready-to-roll icing) (see
Sugarcraft Techniques)

Small and medium pointed
blossom cutters

Small pearl dragées (sugar balls)

METHOD

1. Preheat the oven to 160°C
(fan)/180°C/350°F/Gas Mark 4. Fill a piping
(pastry) bag fitted with an 18mm (¾in)
nozzle (tip) with the chilled choux pastry.
Pipe 15cm (6in) éclairs onto a baking sheet
lined with non-stick baking (parchment)
paper or a silicone liner (bake-o-glide).
Spray the éclairs lightly with vegetable or
sunflower oil and bake in the oven for 50
minutes until golden brown. Transfer to a
wire rack and allow to cool completely.

2. Roll out the yellow sugarpaste and
cut out two medium-pointed five-petal
blossoms for each éclair. Roll out the lime
green and cut one small blossom for each.
Using a cocktail stick (toothpick), imprint
lines along each petal. Set the yellow
blossoms on top of each other, slightly
offsetting the petals, and place the green
blossom in the centre. Carefully pick up
the pieces and pinch together gently from
the back to ruffle the petals. Set aside
to dry in the recesses of an egg box.

ASSEMBLY

1. Whisk the prepared tropical
crème patissière with an electric
hand mixer until smooth.

2. Split each éclair with a sharp
serrated knife (see Filling, Dipping &
Splitting) and spoon the tropical crème
patissière into the base of each.

3. Top the crème patissière with
a mix of sliced tropical fruits.

4. Warm the orange fondant glaze gently
until of a dipping consistency and place
in an open shallow bowl. Dip the top
of each éclair in the fondant to coat
and place on top of the fruit filling.

5. Apply a dab of water to the centres
of the flowers and sprinkle on the
dragées. Add a tropical flower to
the top of each éclair and serve.

CLASSIC CHOCOLATE

Makes 10–12 x 15cm
(6in) éclairs

INGREDIENTS

1 x quantity choux pastry
(see How to Make Éclairs)

1 x quantity vanilla
crème patissière
(see Filling & Topping Recipes)

1 x quantity dark
chocolate ganache
(see Filling & Topping Recipes)

METHOD

1. Preheat the oven to160°C
(fan)/180°C/350°F/Gas Mark 4. Fill a piping
(pastry) bag fitted with an 18mm (¾in)
nozzle (tip) with the chilled choux pastry.
Pipe 15cm (6in) éclairs onto a baking sheet
lined with non-stick baking (parchment)
paper or a silicone liner (bake-o-glide).
Spray the éclairs lightly with vegetable
oil and bake in the preheated oven for 50
minutes until golden brown. Transfer to a
wire rack and allow to cool completely.

ASSEMBLY

1. Pierce the base of each éclair
three times, once at each end
and once in the middle.

2. Beat the chilled vanilla crème patissière
with an electric hand mixer until smooth.
Place in a piping (pastry) bag fitted with a
Bismarck or doughnut filling nozzle (tip).

3. Fill each éclair with crème patissière
(see Filling, Dipping & Splitting).

4. Warm the dark chocolate ganache
gently until it is of a dipping consistency
and place in a shallow bowl at least
as wide as the length of the éclairs.
Dip the top of each éclair in the
ganache to coat and transfer to a
wire rack to allow to set. Serve.

SUGAR & SPICE

Makes 15 x 10cm
(4in) éclairs

INGREDIENTS

1 x quantity choux pastry
(see How to Make Éclairs)

1 x quantity chocolate ginger
chocolate crème patissière
(see Filling & Topping Recipes)

1 x quantity dark
chocolate ganache
(see Filling & Topping Recipes)

Decorations

15g (½oz) crystallized ginger

Pinch of gold edible lustre dust

METHOD

1. Preheat the oven to160°C
(fan)/180°C/350°F/Gas Mark 4. Fill a piping
(pastry) bag fitted with an 18mm (¾in)
nozzle (tip) with the chilled choux pastry.
Pipe 10cm (4in) éclairs onto a baking sheet
lined with non-stick baking (parchment)
paper or a silicone liner (bake-o-glide).
Spray the éclairs lightly with vegetable
oil and bake in the preheated oven for
40 minutes until golden brown. Transfer to
a wire rack and allow to cool completely.

2. Finely dice the crystallized stem ginger
and place in a small bowl with a pinch
of gold lustre dust. Toss well to coat all
the ginger with gold. Set to one side.

ASSEMBLY

1. Pierce the base of each éclair
twice, once at each end.

2. Beat the chilled ginger chocolate crème
patissière with an electric hand mixer until
smooth. Place in a piping (pastry) bag
fitted with a Bismarck filling nozzle (tip).

3. Fill each éclair with crème patissière
(see Filling, Dipping & Splitting).

4. Warm the dark chocolate ganache
gently to a pourable consistency and place
in an open shallow bowl, at least as wide
as the length of the éclairs. Dip the top of
each éclair in the chocolate ganache and
transfer to a wire rack. Add a scattering
of golden ginger down the length of
each éclair and allow to set. Serve.

NUTTY CRUNCH

Makes 18 x 10cm
(4in) éclairs

INGREDIENTS

1 x quantity choux pastry
(see How to Make Éclairs)

1 x quantity nutty choc
crème patissière (see Filling
& Topping Recipes)

Decorations

30g (1oz) whole almonds

30g (1oz) whole hazelnuts

30g (1oz) chopped mixed nuts

50g (1¾oz) dark (semisweet)
chocolate, melted

METHOD

1. Preheat the oven to 160°C
(fan)/180°C/350°F/Gas Mark 4. Fill a piping
(pastry) bag fitted with an 18mm (¾in)
nozzle (tip) with the chilled choux pastry.
Pipe 10cm (4in) éclairs onto a baking sheet
lined with non-stick baking (parchment)
paper or a silicone liner (bake-o-glide).
Spray the éclairs lightly with vegetable
or sunflower oil and bake in the oven for
40 minutes until golden brown. Transfer to
a wire rack and allow to cool completely.

2. Roughly chop the whole almonds
and hazelnuts and toss together
with the chopped mixed nuts.

ASSEMBLY

1. Whisk the prepared nutty choc crème
patissière with an electric hand mixer
until smooth and place in a piping
(pastry) bag fitted with a filling nozzle
(tip) such as a Bismarck or Wilton 230.

2. Pierce the base of each éclair once at
each end and fill with nutty choc crème
patissière (see Filling, Dipping & Splitting).

3. Drizzle the top of each éclair
with the melted dark chocolate and
scatter over the nuts. Serve.

CAFÉ MOCHA

Makes 12 x 12cm
(4¾in) éclairs

INGREDIENTS

1 x quantity choux pastry
(see How to Make Éclairs)

1 x quantity mocha
crème patissière (see
Filling & Topping Recipes)

1 x quantity coffee-
flavoured fondant glaze
(see Filling & Topping Recipes)

Decorations
50g (1¾oz) dark
chocolate, melted

24 chocolate-coated coffee beans

METHOD

1. Preheat the oven to160°C
(fan)/180°C/350°F/Gas Mark 4. Fill a
piping (pastry) bag fitted with an 18mm
(¾in) nozzle (tip) with the chilled choux
pastry. Pipe 12cm (4¾in) éclairs onto
a baking sheet lined with non-stick
baking (parchment) paper or a silicone
liner (bake-o-glide). Spray the éclairs
lightly with vegetable oil and bake in
the preheated oven for 45 minutes
until golden brown. Transfer to a wire
rack and allow to cool completely.

ASSEMBLY

1. Pierce the base of each éclair
twice, once at each end.

2. Beat the chilled mocha crème
patissière with an electric hand
mixer until smooth. Place in a
piping (pastry) bag fitted with a
Bismarck filling nozzle (tip).

3. Fill each éclair with mocha
crème patissière (see Filling,
Dipping & Splitting).

4. Gently warm the coffee glaze to
a pourable consistency and place in
a shallow bowl at least as wide as the
length of the éclairs. Dip the top of each
éclair in the glaze to coat and transfer to
a wire rack. Allow the glaze to set for 5
minutes before adding further decoration.

5. Melt the dark chocolate and allow to
cool slightly. Place in a small disposable
piping (pastry) bag and snip off the
end. Pipe a swirl along the length of the
coffee glaze (see Piping Techniques).
Allow the chocolate to set for 5 minutes
before placing 2 chocolate coffee beans
at one end of each éclair. Serve.

☙ TIP ❧

Letting the coffee fondant and
piped chocolate set a little before
proceeding with the next step
of the decoration will prevent
each element from sliding off!

CHOCOLATE ORANGE

Makes 15 x 12cm
(4¾in) éclairs

INGREDIENTS

1 x quantity choux pastry
(see How to Make Éclairs)

1 x quantity chocolate orange
crème patissière (see Filling
& Topping Recipes)

1 x quantity milk chocolate
ganache (see Filling &
Topping Recipes)

Decoration
Zest of 1 large orange

METHOD

1. Preheat the oven to 160°C
(fan)/180°C/350°F/Gas Mark 4. Fill a
piping (pastry) bag fitted with an 18mm
(¾in) nozzle (tip) with the chilled choux
pastry. Pipe 12cm (4¾in) éclairs onto
a baking sheet lined with non-stick
baking (parchment) paper or a silicone
liner (bake-o-glide). Spray the éclairs
lightly with vegetable or sunflower oil
and bake in the oven for 45 minutes
until golden brown. Transfer to a wire
rack and allow to cool completely.

2. Zest the orange peel into
long lengths (see Tip).

ASSEMBLY

1. Whisk the prepared chocolate orange
crème patissière with an electric hand
whisk until smooth and place in a piping
(pastry) bag fitted with a filling nozzle (tip).

2. Pierce the base of each éclair
three times. Fill each with chocolate
orange crème patissière (see
Filling, Dipping & Splitting).

3. Warm the milk chocolate ganache
gently until of a dipping consistency and
place in an open shallow bowl. Dip the
tops of the éclairs in the ganache to coat.

4. Wind orange zest around a skewer
or cocktail stick and hold in position
for 1 minute. Release the twirls, cut
to required size and add a twirl to
the top of each éclair. Serve.

TIP

It is best to remove the rind of
the orange using a zester or a
julienne peeler. Hold it firmly
against the side of the orange
and move it slowly across the
skin, rotating the orange in your
hand as you move the zester.
It will take a little practice to
judge the pressure needed to
get long lengths for twirling –
just work on fresh areas of the
orange skin as you practise,
avoiding the bitter white pith.

COCONUT PARADISE

Makes 15 x 12cm
(4¾in) éclairs

INGREDIENTS

1 x quantity choux pastry
(see How to Make Éclairs)

1 x quantity coconut
crème patissière (see Filling
& Topping Recipes)

1 x quantity dark chocolate
ganache (see Filling &
Topping Recipes)

15ml (1 tbsp) coconut liqueur

Decoration
100g (3½oz)
desiccated coconut

METHOD

1. Preheat the oven to 160°C
(fan)/180°C/350°F/Gas Mark 4. Fill a
piping (pastry) bag fitted with an 18mm
(¾in) nozzle (tip) with the chilled choux
pastry. Pipe 12cm (4¾in) éclairs onto
a baking sheet lined with non-stick
baking (parchment) paper or a silicone
liner (bake-o-glide). Spray the éclairs
lightly with vegetable or sunflower oil
and bake in the oven for 45 minutes
until golden brown. Transfer to a wire
rack and allow to cool completely.

2. Place the desiccated coconut
in a shallow open bowl.

ASSEMBLY

1. Whisk the chilled coconut crème
patissière with an electric hand whisk
until smooth and place in a piping (pastry)
bag fitted with a filling nozzle (tip).

2. Pierce the base of each éclair once
at each end and fill with coconut crème
patissière (see Filling, Dipping & Splitting).

3. Warm the dark chocolate ganache
gently until of a dipping consistency.
Transfer to an open shallow bowl
and beat in the coconut liqueur. Dip
the tops of the éclairs in the ganache
to coat and then dip straight into
the desiccated coconut. Serve.

CHOC CHERRY

Makes 10–12 x 15cm
(6in) éclairs

INGREDIENTS

1 x quantity choux pastry
(see How to Make Éclairs)

1 x quantity choc cherry filling
(see Fillings & Topping Recipes)

250g (9oz) pitted cherries

1 x quantity milk chocolate
ganache (see Filling &
Topping Recipes)

Decorations

Pale pink sugarpaste (rolled
fondant/ready-to-roll icing)
(see Sugarcraft Techniques)

Pink and orange edible
lustre dusts

Rejuvenator fluid or clear alcohol

METHOD

1. Preheat the oven to 160°C
(fan)/180°C/350°F/Gas Mark 4. Fill a piping
(pastry) bag fitted with an 18mm (¾in)
nozzle (tip) with the chilled choux pastry.
Pipe 15cm (6in) éclairs onto a baking sheet
lined with non-stick baking (parchment)
paper or a silicone liner (bake-o-glide).
Spray the éclairs lightly with vegetable
or sunflower oil and bake in the oven for
50 minutes until golden brown. Transfer to
a wire rack and allow to cool completely.

2. Halve the pitted cherries and set aside.

3. Roll out the pale pink sugarpaste
and using a cutter, cut out a large and
small cherry blossom for each éclair.
Shape using your fingertips (see
Sugarcraft Techniques) and set aside
to dry in the recesses of an egg tray.

ASSEMBLY

1. Place the chocolate cherry cream
filling in a large piping (pastry) bag
fitted with an open star nozzle tip.

2. Split each éclair with a sharp serrated
knife and pipe the chocolate cherry
cream filling into the base of each
(see Filling, Dipping & Splitting). Top
with a line of halved pitted cherries.

3. Warm the milk chocolate ganache
gently until it is of a soft spreadable
consistency. Using a palette knife,
coat the tops of each éclair with the
ganache and set onto the bases.

4. Dust the centres of the blossoms with
a little pink lustre dust. Mix the orange
lustre dust together with rejuvenator
fluid or clear alcohol and using a fine
paintbrush paint in the centres of each
blossom (see Sugarcraft Techniques). Add
one large and one small cherry blossom
flower to the top of each éclair. Serve.

BITTERSWEET MINIS

Makes 32 x 7cm
(2¾in) éclairs

INGREDIENTS

1 x quantity choux pastry
(see How to Make Éclairs)

1 x quantity dark chocolate
ganache (see Filling & Topping
Recipes) made with 400ml
(14fl oz) double (heavy)
cream and 300g (10½oz)
dark (semisweet) chocolate

350g (12oz) dark (semisweet)
chocolate, melted

METHOD

1. Preheat the oven to 160°C
(fan)/180°C/350°F/Gas Mark 4. Fill a
piping (pastry) bag fitted with a 1cm
(½in) wide serrated nozzle (tip) with the
chilled choux pastry. Pipe 7cm (2¾in)
éclairs onto a baking sheet lined with
non-stick baking (parchment) paper or
a silicone liner (bake-o-glide). Spray the
éclairs lightly with vegetable or sunflower
oil and bake in the oven for 35 minutes
until golden brown. Transfer to a wire
rack and allow to cool completely.

TIP

Chocolate ganache (of all
varieties) can be used as a
filling as well as a topping, but it
is very rich so is best reserved
for the smallest éclairs.

ASSEMBLY

1. Split each éclair with a sharp serrated
knife (see Filling, Dipping & Splitting).

2. Prepare the ganache to be used as the
filling. It needs to be the consistency of
peanut butter – soft enough to pipe but
still firm enough to hold its shape. Place
it in a piping (pastry) bag fitted with a
1cm (½in) serrated open nozzle (tip).
Pipe onto the base of each éclair using a
circular motion to create a swirled look.

3. Put the melted dark chocolate
into an open shallow bowl at least
as wide as the éclairs and dip the
top of each éclair to coat.

4. Set the tops onto the bases and allow
the chocolate topping to set. Serve.

OOH LA LA, CHOCOLAT!

MALTED MILK

Makes 10–12 x 15cm (6in) éclairs

INGREDIENTS

1 x quantity choux pastry (see How to Make Éclairs)

1 x quantity malted milk crème patissière (see Filling & Topping Recipes)

1 x quantity milk chocolate ganache (see Filling & Topping Recipes)

Decoration

120g (4½oz) malted chocolate balls such as Maltesers or Whoppers

METHOD

1. Preheat the oven to 160°C (fan)/180°C/350°F/Gas Mark 4. Fill a piping (pastry) bag fitted with an 18mm (¾in) nozzle (tip) with the chilled choux pastry. Pipe 15cm (6in) éclairs onto a baking sheet lined with non-stick baking (parchment) paper or a silicone liner (bake-o-glide). Spray the éclairs lightly with vegetable or sunflower oil and bake in the oven for 50 minutes until golden brown. Transfer to a wire rack and allow to cool completely.

2. Roughly chop the malted chocolate balls.

ASSEMBLY

1. Whisk the chilled malted milk crème patissière with an electric hand whisk until smooth and place in a piping (pastry) bag fitted with a filling nozzle (tip).

2. Pierce the base of each éclair three times, once at each end and once in the middle. Fill each with the malted milk crème patissière (see Filling, Dipping & Splitting).

3. Warm the milk chocolate ganache until it is of dipping consistency and place in shallow bowl. Dip the top of each éclair in the ganache to coat and then sprinkle with the roughly chopped malted chocolate balls. Serve.

CHOUX ALLUMETTES

Makes 36 x 16cm
(6¼in) sticks

INGREDIENTS

½ x quantity choux pastry
(see How to Make Éclairs)

100g (3½oz) dark
(semisweet) chocolate

Decorations

2 tbsp nibbed sugar

Multicoloured sprinkles
(nonpareils)

METHOD

1. Preheat the oven to 160°C
(fan)/180°C/350°F/Gas Mark 4. Fill a
piping (pastry) bag fitted with a 5mm
(³⁄₁₆in) open serrated nozzle (tip) with
the chilled choux pastry. Pipe 16cm
(6¼in) éclairs onto a baking sheet lined
with non-stick baking (parchment)
paper or a silicone liner (bake-o-glide).

2. Spray the sticks lightly with
vegetable oil before scattering half
of them with nibbed sugar. Bake in
the oven for 25 minutes until crisp and
golden. Allow to cool on the baking
tray for 5 minutes before transferring
to a wire rack to cool completely.

ASSEMBLY

1. Chop the chocolate into small pieces
and place in a heatproof bowl above a
pan or steaming water to melt, or melt
in the microwave in short 30-second
bursts, stirring well after each burst.

2. Dip the ends of the unsugared
sticks into the melted chocolate and
scatter with multicoloured sprinkles.
Set to dry on a sheet of non-stick
baking (parchment) paper. Serve.

 TIP

Just as you can pipe long
sticks like this in choux pastry,
you can also pipe letters,
words and names. Make a
card template of the letters
you wish to write and place it
underneath a sheet of non-stick
baking (parchment) paper to
use as a guide when piping.

DOUBLE-CHOC BUNS

Makes 16 buns

INGREDIENTS

1 x quantity chocolate
choux pastry (see How
to Make Éclairs)

1 litre (1¾ pints)
vanilla ice cream

300g (10½oz)
white chocolate

Decorations

50g (1¾oz) white
chocolate curls

2 tbsp dark (semisweet)
chocolate sprinkles
(nonpareils)

METHOD

1. Preheat the oven to 160°C
(fan)/180°C/350°F/Gas Mark 4. Fill a
piping (pastry) bag fitted with an 18mm
(¾in) nozzle (tip) with the chilled choux
pastry and pipe in rounds, each about
4.5cm in diameter, onto a baking sheet
lined with non-stick baking (parchment)
paper or a silicone liner (bake-o-glide).
Spray the buns lightly with vegetable or
sunflower oil and bake in the oven for 40
minutes until golden brown. Transfer to a
wire rack and allow to cool completely.

✎ TIP ✎

You can buy chocolate curls in
the supermarket but they are
easy to make yourself. Take a bar
of chocolate and use a vegetable
peeler or sharp flat-bladed knife
to scrape along the flat side of
the chocolate, working towards
you, to form small curls. For small
curls, keep the strokes short and
for larger curls use longer strokes.

ASSEMBLY

1. Cut the top third from each choux bun
with a sharp serrated knife. Scoop out
any webbed choux from the middle.

2. Add a scoop of vanilla ice cream
to each and replace the lids. Place
in the freezer for 30 minutes.

3. Meanwhile, melt the white chocolate.
Chop into pieces and melt in a heatproof
bowl over a pan of steaming water or
in the microwave in short 30-second
bursts, stirring after each burst.

4. Toss together the white chocolate
curls and dark chocolate sprinkles
in a small bowl. Dip the top of each
bun into the melted chocolate and
top with the curls and sprinkles.

5. Place the buns in the freezer and
remove 10 minutes before serving.

WHITE HEAVEN

Makes 10–12 x 15cm
(6in) éclairs

INGREDIENTS

1 x quantity choux pastry
(see How to Make Éclairs)

50g (1¾oz) dark
(semisweet) chocolate

1 x quantity white chocolate
crème patissière (see Filling
& Topping Recipes)

1 x quantity white chocolate
ganache (see Filling &
Topping Recipes)

Decorations

50g (1¾oz) white
chocolate curls

METHOD

1. Preheat the oven to 160°C
(fan)/180°C/350°F/Gas Mark 4. Fill a piping
(pastry) bag fitted with an 18mm (¾in)
nozzle (tip) with the chilled choux pastry.
Pipe 15cm (6in) éclairs onto a baking sheet
lined with non-stick baking (parchment)
paper or a silicone liner (bake-o-glide).
Spray the éclairs lightly with vegetable or
sunflower oil and bake in the oven for 50
minutes until golden brown. Transfer to a
wire rack and allow to cool completely.

2. Melt the dark chocolate. Chop the
chocolate into small pieces and place in
a heatproof bowl. Place the bowl over the
top of pan of steaming water and allow to
melt stirring occasionally. Alternatively,
melt in the microwave in short 30-second
bursts, stirring well after each burst.

ASSEMBLY

1. Whisk the prepared white
chocolate crème patissière with an
electric hand whisk until smooth
and place in a piping (pastry) bag
fitted with a filling nozzle (tip).

2. Pierce the base of each éclair
three times, once at each end and
once in the middle. Fill each with
white chocolate crème patissière
(see Filling, Dipping & Splitting).

3. Warm the white chocolate ganache
gently until of a dipping consistency and
place in an open shallow bowl. Dip the
tops of the éclairs in the ganache to coat.

4. Place the melted dark chocolate in
a small piping (pastry) bag and pipe
three thin lines along the length of
each éclair (see Piping Techniques).

5. Top each éclair with a scattering
of white chocolate curls. Serve.

CHOUX CREATIONS

SALTED CARAMEL PROFITEROLES

Makes 42 profiteroles
(serves 6)

INGREDIENTS

1 x quantity choux pastry
(see How to Make Éclairs)

1 x quantity vanilla Chantilly
cream made with 300ml
(10fl oz) double (heavy) cream
(see Filling & Topping Recipes)

Chocolate Sauce

100g (3½oz) dark
(semisweet) chocolate

35g (1¼oz) butter

15g (1 tbsp) golden (corn) syrup

30ml (2 tbsp) water

Salted Caramel Sauce

70g (2½oz) caster
(superfine) sugar

25g (1oz) soft light brown sugar

45g (1½oz) golden syrup

100ml (3½fl oz) double
(heavy) cream

25g (1oz) butter

½ tsp vanilla extract

½ tsp ground sea salt

METHOD

1. Preheat the oven to 160°C
(fan)/180°C/350°F/Gas Mark 4. Fill a piping
(pastry) bag fitted with a 15mm (⅝in) round
open nozzle (tip) with the chilled choux
pastry. Pipe into rounds each approximately
3.5cm (1⅜in) diameter onto a baking sheet
lined with non-stick baking (parchment)
paper or a silicone liner (bake-o-glide).

～ TIP ～
Once filled, profiteroles are
best eaten the same day.

2. Flatten any peaks on the top of the rounds with your fingertip, dipping in a little water first to prevent it from sticking. Spray lightly with vegetable or sunflower oil and bake in the oven for 35 minutes until golden brown. Transfer to a wire rack and allow to cool completely.

3. Prepare the chocolate sauce. Heat the chocolate, butter and syrup gently in a heatproof bowl over a pan of steaming water until completely melted. Stir to combine evenly. Add 30ml (2 tbsp) of water and mix again. Transfer to a jug for serving.

❦ TIP ❦

Adding the water in step 3 helps to keep the chocolate sauce liquid. If it has been made in advance and firms too much before serving, simply heat gently.

4. To make the salted caramel sauce, place the caster (superfine) sugar, soft light brown sugar and syrup in a pan and gently heat, stirring occasionally, until the sugar is completely dissolved. Add the cream, butter and vanilla and continue to heat, stirring occasionally, until the mixture comes to the boil. Simmer for 2–3 minutes, remove from the heat and stir in the sea salt. Transfer to a jug for serving.

Assembly

1. Pierce the base of each profiterole with a small piping tip. Place the vanilla Chantilly cream in a disposable piping (pastry) bag and snip off about 1cm (½in) from the end. Insert the end of the piping (pastry) bag into the profiterole through the hole and squeeze to fill. Chill the filled profiteroles in the fridge until serving.

2. When ready to serve, divide the profiteroles into one large or several individual bowls. Pour or drizzle over the chocolate sauce, followed by the salted caramel sauce. Serve.

FRUIT BASKETS

Makes 8 baskets

INGREDIENTS

I x quantity choux pastry (see How to Make Éclairs)

I x quantity of vanilla Chantilly cream, made with 250ml (9fl oz) double (heavy) cream (see Filling & Topping Recipes)

230g (8oz) fresh mixed fruit such as grapes and strawberries (chopped), blueberries and raspberries, tossed together

Icing (confectioners') sugar, to dust

METHOD

1. Preheat the oven to 160°C (fan)/180°C/350°F/Gas Mark 4. Fill a disposable piping (pastry) bag with the chilled choux pastry. Snip the end off the bag approximately 1cm (½in) up from the end and pipe 10 handle shapes (2 extra to allow for breakage) onto a baking sheet lined with non-stick baking (parchment) paper or a silicone liner (bake-o-glide). The handles should be roughly 5cm (2in) wide and 12cm (4¾in) long. Spray lightly with vegetable or sunflower oil and bake for 15 minutes until crisp and golden. Transfer to a wire rack and allow to cool completely.

2. Fit another piping (pastry) bag with a 1.5cm (⅝in) serrated open nozzle (tip). Cut a further 4cm (1½in) from the piping bag filled with choux and drop this bag inside the new bag. On a separate lined baking sheet, pipe large bulbs of choux to create the baskets, approximately 5cm (2in) wide and 4.5cm (1¾in) tall. Spray lightly with vegetable or sunflower oil and bake in the oven for 50 minutes. Allow to cool for 5 minutes.

ASSEMBLY

1. Take the top off the choux balls with a sharp serrated knife to form the baskets. Scoop out any webbed choux, then place back on the baking sheet and bake for another 10 minutes to crisp the insides. Transfer to a wire rack and allow to cool completely.

2. Spoon the vanilla Chantilly cream into the base of the baskets and add a little of the mixed fruit.

3. Set the handles inside the baskets, pressing the ends into the cream to secure. Top up each basket with the remaining fruit. Dust with icing (confectioners') sugar. Serve.

CHOC-ICE HEARTS

Makes 16 hearts

INGREDIENTS

1 x quantity choux pastry
(see How to Make Éclairs)

500ml (18fl oz)
vanilla ice cream

450g (1lb) dark (semisweet)
chocolate, melted

50g (1¾oz) white
chocolate, melted

EQUIPMENT

Wooden lolly sticks

METHOD

1. Preheat the oven to 160°C
(fan)/180°C/350°F/Gas Mark 4. Fill a
piping (pastry) bag fitted with a 1.5cm
(⅝in) serrated open nozzle (tip) with
the chilled choux pastry. Pipe V shapes,
with each length of the V approximately
6.5cm (2½in), onto a baking sheet lined
with non-stick baking (parchment)
paper or a silicone liner (bake-o-glide).

2. Dip your fingertips in water and
gently push the tops of the Vs down
approximately 1cm (½in) to make slightly
fatter at the top. Spray lightly with
vegetable oil and bake in the oven for 45
minutes until golden brown. Transfer to a
wire rack and allow to cool completely.

ASSEMBLY

1. Split the choux hearts in half using a sharp serrated knife. Scoop out any webbed choux from the inside.

3. Set the tops of the choux hearts back on and insert a wooden lolly stick into the bottom of the heart, right into the ball of ice cream. Set the hearts onto a baking sheet lined with non-stick baking (parchment) paper and place in the freezer for 1 hour.

2. Place three small balls of ice cream into the choux hearts, one sitting at the base of the V and one each in the top parts of the heart.

❧ TIP ❧

Choc-Ice Hearts can be stored in the freezer in a sealed container or freezer bag for up to one month and served as and when needed.

4. To coat with melted chocolate, remove four hearts from the freezer one at a time. Dip first one side into the melted dark chocolate and then the other.

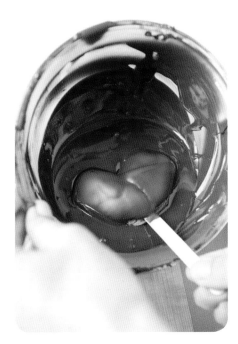

5. Set the heart back down onto the lined baking tray. Coat all four hearts, returning them to the freezer when you are ready to coat the next batch.

6. To add the white chocolate heart detail, melt the white chocolate, place in a small piping (pastry) bag and snip off the end. Pipe a double scribbly freehand heart onto the flatter side of each choc ice and store in the freezer until ready to serve.

CHOUX CREATIONS

CHOC HONEYCOMB CHEESECAKE

Makes I x 20cm (8in)
cheesecake (serves 12)

INGREDIENTS

2 x quantities choux pastry
(see How to Make Éclairs)

Cheesecake Filling

750g (Ilb 10oz) cream cheese

160g (5¾oz) icing
(confectioners') sugar

10ml (2 tsp) vanilla extract

675ml (1¼ pints) double
(heavy) cream

3 x chocolate honeycomb
bars such as Crunchie,
roughly chopped

Decorations

100g (3½oz) grated dark
(semisweet) chocolate

I x chocolate honeycomb
bar, roughly chopped

25g (1oz) dark (semisweet)
chocolate chips

EQUIPMENT

3 x baking sheets

Baking (parchment) paper

20cm (8in) dessert ring

Electric hand whisk

Acetate sheet (or strips cut from
A4 sheet), to line dessert ring

⤳ TIP ⤳

If you don't have a dessert
ring, use the side of a
20cm (8in) springform tin.

METHOD

1. Line three baking sheets with non-stick
baking (parchment) paper. On the reverse
side of each piece of the paper draw a
circle in pencil 16.5cm (6½in) in diameter.

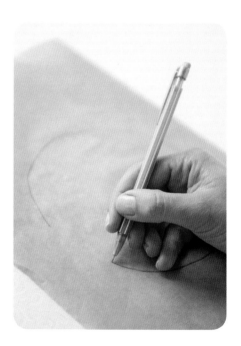

2. Preheat the oven to 160°C (fan)/180°C/350°F/Gas Mark 4. Fill a piping (pastry) bag fitted with a 1.5cm (⅝in) open nozzle (tip) with the chilled choux pastry. Pipe a spiral, starting in the centre to fill each of the 16.5cm (6½in) circles. Spray lightly with vegetable oil and bake in the oven for 1 hour. Allow the discs to cool on the trays for 10 minutes before transferring to a wire rack to cool completely.

4. Reserve 250g (9oz) of the cheesecake filling and set aside. Mix the chopped honeycomb chocolate bars into the remainder with a wooden spoon.

5. Trim the three choux discs to exactly 20cm (8in) circles either by pressing the dessert ring over it to cut away the excess or trimming to size with a sharp knife.

3. To prepare the cheesecake filling, beat together the cream cheese and icing (confectioners') sugar with an electric hand whisk until just combined. Whisk in the vanilla extract followed by the cream, a little at a time, and continue to whisk until the mixture stands in medium-firm peaks.

Assembly

1. Line the dessert ring with acetate or non-stick baking (parchment) paper, allowing the paper to rise 5cm (2in) above the top of the ring. Set the ring onto a serving plate and place one choux disc into the base.

2. Top with half of the cheesecake and honeycomb filling. Add a further choux disc and then the remaining cheesecake mixture. Top with the final choux disc, pressing it down to an even level.

3. Chill in the fridge for 30 minutes. Once chilled, carefully remove the dessert ring and acetate.

4. Cover the edges of a serving plate with cling film (plastic wrap).

5. Cover the top and sides of the cheesecake with the reserved 250g (9oz) plain cheesecake mixture, spreading it evenly with a palette knife.

6. To coat the sides of the cheesecake with grated dark chocolate, hold the grated chocolate in a cupped hand and press gently against the sides. Scatter the chopped honeycomb and choc chips over the top, remove the excess grated chocolate and the cling film (plastic wrap) from the plate. Serve.

✺ TIP ✺

Piping a 16.5cm (6½in) circle will create a 20cm (8in) finished disc.

PECAN STREUSEL BUNS

Makes 16 buns

INGREDIENTS

1 x quantity choux pastry
(see How to Make Éclairs)

Butterscotch Crème Patissière

150g (5½oz) light
muscovado sugar

125g (4½oz) butter

6 egg yolks

50g (1¾oz) cornflour (cornstarch)

750ml (2½fl oz) whole milk

7.5ml (1½ tsp) vanilla extract

Pecan Streusel

40g (1½oz) pecans

75g (2¾oz) light muscovado sugar

45g (1¾oz) plain
(all-purpose) flour

Pinch of salt

60g (2¼oz) butter, cold diced

METHOD

1. Prepare the butterscotch crème patissière. Place half of the light muscovado sugar (75g/2¾oz) in a saucepan with the butter. Heat gently to melt the butter, stirring occasionally. Continue to heat the mixture gently until the crystals in the sugar have melted and you can't feel them in the base of the pan with your spoon. Remove from the heat and set aside.

2. In a large jug or batter bowl, whisk together the egg yolks and remaining muscovado sugar until even. Add the cornflour (corn starch) and whisk well again. Set aside.

3. Whisk the milk slowly into the butter and sugar mixture in the pan and add the vanilla. Heat until just below boiling point.

4. Remove from the heat and pour slowly into the egg mixture, whisking continuously until the two are fully combined. Return the mixture to the pan and heat, continuing to whisk until the mixture thickens and comes to the boil. Cook for a further 2 minutes. Remove from the heat and transfer to a clean bowl.

5. Cover the top of the butterscotch crème patissiere with a sheet of cling film (plastic wrap), placing it directly on the surface to prevent a skin from forming. Allow to cool to room temperature, then place in the fridge to chill completely.

6. Prepare the streusel mixture. Blitz the pecans in a food processor until finely ground and no large chunks remain. Combine the ground pecans with the sugar, flour and salt in a bowl. Add the cold diced butter and rub in until the mixture is even.

7. Tip the crumbly mixture out onto a sheet of cling film (plastic wrap). Top with a further sheet of cling film and with a rolling pin, roll to a depth of 4mm ($\frac{3}{16}$in), compacting the mixture together into a solid sheet. Transfer the cling film to a tray (baking sheet or chopping board) and place in the freezer for 1 hour to harden.

ASSEMBLY

1. Preheat the oven to 160°C (fan)/180°C/350°F/Gas Mark 4. Place the chilled choux in a piping bag fitted with a 1.5cm (⅝in) round open nozzle. Pipe 16 balls of choux, about 4cm (1½in) in diameter (well spaced to allow for spreading) onto a baking tray lined with non-stick baking (parchment) paper or a silicone line (bake-o-glide).

2. Remove the streusel mixture from the freezer and using a 3.5cm (1⅜in) cutter (just slightly smaller than the size of the choux) cut out 16 discs. Place one on top of each piped choux ball.

3. Bake in the oven for 40 minutes until dark golden. Transfer to a wire rack to cool completely.

4. Beat the chilled butterscotch crème patissière well with an electric hand mixer until of a smooth and even consistency. Place in a large disposable piping (pastry) bag.

5. Pierce the side of each streusel bun with a piping tip or sharp knife. Snip the end from the disposable piping (pastry) bag and fill each bun with butterscotch crème patissière. Serve.

CROQUEMBOUCHE

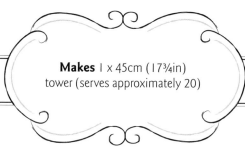

Makes I x 45cm (17¾in)
tower (serves approximately 20)

INGREDIENTS

3 x quantities choux pastry
(see How to Make Éclairs)

2 x quantities crème patissière
(see Filling & Topping Recipes),
plus 100g (3½oz) diced butter

Caramel (to coat tops
and assemble)

600g (1lb 5oz) caster
(superfine) sugar

180g (6oz) liquid glucose
syrup or golden (corn)
syrup if difficult to obtain

120ml (4fl oz) water

Caramel (for spun sugar)

150g (5½oz) caster
(superfine) sugar

45g (1½oz) liquid glucose syrup

30ml (2 tbsp) water

Decorations

Gumpaste roses – approx.
8 x white and 8 x purple
(see Sugarcraft Techniques)

Silver heart dragées

Tiny silver dragées (sugar balls)

EQUIPMENT

Heavy-bottomed saucepan

Food thermometer

38cm (15in) polystyrene cone
(these can be bought from
most good craft suppliers)

Rolling pin or the handle
of a wooden spoon

2 x forks

METHOD

1. Prepare the crème patissière following
the instructions up to step 4, then remove
the pan from the heat and stir through
100g (3½oz) diced butter. This helps give
the crème patissière a firm set. Transfer
to a clean bowl and contact cover with
cling film (plastic wrap). Allow to cool to
room temperature, then chill until firm.

2. Preheat the oven to 160°C
(fan)/180°C/350°F/Gas Mark 4. Fill a
piping (pastry) bag fitted with a 1.5cm
(⅝in) round open nozzle (tip) with
the prepared chilled choux pastry.

 TIP

Croquembouches are best
served the same day as
constructed, as the caramel
will soften if stored in the
fridge for any length of time.

3. Pipe balls, 4cm (1½in) in diameter, onto a baking sheet lined with non-stick baking (parchment) paper or a silicone liner (bake-o-glide). Hold the piping (pastry) bag 1cm (½in) above the tray and pipe until the choux reaches the correct size. Stop squeezing the bag and move the tip quickly away horizontally. Flatten any peaks in the choux with a dampened fingertip, spray lightly with vegetable or sunflower oil and bake in the oven for 50 minutes until golden brown. Transfer to a wire rack and allow to cool completely.

4. Beat the chilled crème patissière with an electric hand mixer until smooth and place in a disposable piping (pastry) bag. Set out a long length of baking (parchment) paper. Pierce the base of each choux bun with a small piping nozzle (tip). Snip the end from the piping (pastry) bag and fill each bun setting them base down onto the sheet of baking (parchment) paper.

5. Prepare the caramel. Place the sugar, glucose and water in a heavy-bottomed saucepan. Heat over a gentle heat, stirring occasionally, until the sugar has melted. Regularly brush down the sides of the pan with a pastry brush dipped in water to prevent sugar crystals forming. Once the mixture comes to the boil, do not stir. Allow the sugar to boil over a low heat until it reaches 170°C/338°F. Remove from the heat immediately when it reaches temperature. Keeping the heat on low is the best way to stop it from burning. When it is reaching temperature, the sugar will have cleared and just be starting to turn a hint of golden colour – it takes roughly 25 minutes over a low heat.

∾ TIP ∾

The caramel in the pan will begin to set as you work and can be gently reheated until it is molten again. Always heat very gently to avoid the caramel darkening excessively.

6. Prepare a bowl of iced water for your hands should any caramel touch your fingers (hot caramel can cause a serious burn). Lay out a second long sheet of baking (parchment) paper.

7. Take each filled choux bun one at a time and dip the top into the pan of caramel, taking care not to let any filling touch the caramel. Lift out the bun and let the excess drain off. Swipe the edge of the caramel against the side of the pan cutting off any sugar strings and set down onto the clean sheet of baking (parchment) paper. Repeat until all of the buns are coated.

ASSEMBLY

1. Cover the polystyrene cone completely with non-stick baking (parchment) paper and set it onto a sheet of baking (parchment) paper. Spray liberally with cake-release or spray oil.

2. Dip one side of the previously dipped choux buns into the caramel and arrange in a ring around the base of the cone, holding each bun in place for 30 seconds as the caramel hardens to secure it to its neighbour.

3. Build up the tiers in rings, dipping one side of the bun into the caramel and securing it to the top of the bun in the ring below it.

∾ TIP ∾

There will be a small number of choux buns left over after finishing the construction of the tower. But it's better to have too many than not enough, and allows you to select the right bun for the right space as you go along.

4. Work your way upwards, keeping to the shape of the cone until you reach the top. Now check the tower and drizzle in any additional caramel to secure the buns in any weak spots you can see.

5. Allow the caramel to firm for 10 minutes. Meanwhile, prepare a serving plate or board.

6. Carefully tilt the tower, supporting it with your hands, and insert a sharp knife into the base of the polystyrene cone. Twist and remove the cone and paper. Set the croquembouche onto the serving plate.

∽ TIP ∽

You can create much smaller free-form towers simply by arranging the buns on a serving plate and glueing together with caramel to create the tower. Larger croquembouches, however, need the support of a polystyrene cone to construct them successfully.

7. Decorate with gumpaste roses and silver heart dragées, inserting them into the spaces between buns and securing with a little caramel.

8. Prepare the spun sugar to cover the tower. Make up a small batch of fresh caramel, preparing as step 5 in the Method (as it's a smaller quantity it won't take as long). Prepare your work area – spinning sugar can be a messy business, so consider lining the floor with newspaper or even working outside if the weather is dry.

9. Hold two forks firmly back to back. Dip the tips into the caramel and hold the rolling pin in the other hand. Quickly flick the forks backwards and forwards over the rolling pin to create fine strands of sugar.

10. Gently gather the strands together into a ribbon and wind around the croquembouche. Repeat, creating further strands until the tower is decorated as you wish. Sprinkle tiny silver dragées onto the spun sugar ribbon. Serve.

TO CREATE DIFFERENT SIZED TOWERS

Size of finished tower (cone size)	Approx. number of choux buns	Quantity of choux pastry	Quantity of crème patissière (butter)	Quantity of caramel
20cm/8in (free-form)	22	1	1 (50g/1¾oz)	180g/6oz caster (superfine) sugar 55g/2oz glucose 35ml/1¼fl oz water
23cm/9in (free-form)	28	1½	1 (50g/1¾oz)	200g/7oz caster (superfine) sugar 60g/2¼oz glucose 40ml/1¼fl oz water
30cm/12in (25cm/10in)	38	2	1½ (75g/2¾oz)	350g/12oz caster (superfine) sugar 105g/3½oz glucose 70ml/2¼fl oz water
38cm/15in (32cm/12½in)	46	2½	1½ (75g/2¾oz)	500g/1lb 2oz caster (superfine) sugar 150g/5½oz glucose 100ml/3½fl oz water
45cm/17¾in (38cm/15in)	56	3	2 (100g/3½oz)	600g/1lb 5oz caster (superfine) sugar 180g/6oz glucose 120ml/4fl oz water

HOW TO DECORATE

PIPING TECHNIQUES

PIPING DETAIL

For the decoration of éclairs you can pipe detail in melted chocolate, warmed fondant, ganache and royal icing. The principles for piping neatly are the same no matter what you are working with. To fill a piping (pastry) bag, fit the bag inside a large glass or jug, folding the ends over the top edge of the glass or jug – this leaves both hands free to spoon or pour the contents into the bag. Unfold the excess from the top edge of the glass or jug and lift out the filled bag.

LINES

1. Fit your chosen nozzle (tip) or snip off the end of the piping (pastry) bag and fill. Position the nozzle just above the piping starting point on your éclair. Apply an even pressure to the bag. As the icing starts to flow, allow it to 'attach' to the start point.

2. Continually applying pressure, lift the bag up vertically slightly (1cm/½in) and begin to move horizontally in the direction you want the line to go, maintaining the vertical position.

3. To finish, drop the line back down to the surface gently touching the nozzle (tip) down to secure and break off the piping.

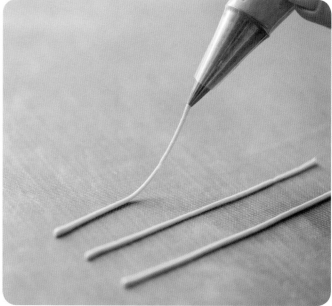

Snail Trail

1. Fit a small piping (pastry) bag with your required nozzle (tip) and fill the bag with royal icing or a medium-firm ganache.

2. Hold the nozzle (tip) at a 45-degree angle to the surface where your trail will start. Squeeze the bag until the icing forms the size of bulb you require. Release the pressure, stopping the squeeze, and then pull the bag away in the direction of the snail trail. This will form the tail of the bulb.

3. Reposition the nozzle 5mm (3/16in) from the first tailed bulb and repeat the process. Squeeze the bag until the bulb joins the previous tail and repeat to form the length of trail required.

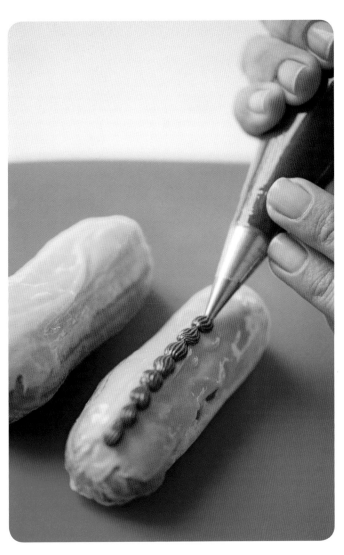

SUGARCRAFT TECHNIQUES

How to Colour Sugarpaste

Edible gel paste colours are the best product to colour sugarpaste (rolled fondant/ready-to-roll icing), gumpaste, fondant and royal icing. They are intensely coloured and only a very small amount will provide a vibrant colour without changing the consistency of your sugarpaste.

1. Knead white sugarpaste till soft and pliable on a work surface lightly dusted with icing (confectioners') sugar.

2. Form into a sausage shape and flatten. Using a cocktail stick (toothpick), add the gel paste colour to the centre of the flattened sugarpaste.

3. Pinch together the edges of the sugarpaste to seal the gel inside. Roll the sausage between your hands to begin to spread the gel from the middle out through the sausage. Keep folding the sausage to bury the colour into the middle again. Repeat until the colour is spread evenly through the sugarpaste.

4. Wrap in cling film (plastic wrap) and allow the colour to develop. This will give the sugarpaste a chance to cool down and firm slightly before use. Colour intensifies over a period of 10 minutes or so. Unwrap and knead gently, checking that the colour is even. Your coloured sugarpaste is now ready to be used.

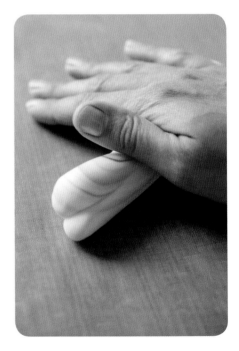

Tips for Working with Sugarpaste

- Very lightly dust the work surface and rolling pin with a little icing (confectioners') sugar to prevent the sugarpaste from sticking as you roll it out. Keep the dusting light otherwise coloured pastes will pick up a dusty sheen.

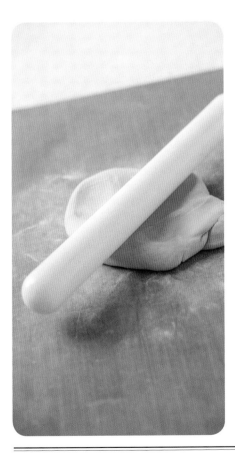

- Any dusty marks can be gently brushed off with a soft clean paintbrush.

- For dark-coloured pastes where you want to avoid any dust, grease the surface and your hands with a little vegetable fat such as Trex.

- Sugarpaste should be kneaded before using to warm and soften it ready for rolling out and prevent it from cracking. You can also microwave it on a clean plate in short 10-second bursts, which will gently soften the paste without it becoming marked with flecks of dust.

- It can be useful to dry rolled-out sugarpaste a little before cutting out shapes by simply letting it sit on the work surface for a couple of minutes. This can also help prevent cut-outs from stretching and pulling out of shape.

- Always check that your rolled-out paste is free-moving and not stuck to the work surface before cutting.

- Dust cutters gently with a sugar duster before using to ensure that the shape you are cutting out doesn't stick to the cutter.

- Cut-out flowers, leaves and other sugarpaste shapes sometimes need to be supported while they dry before using. This also gives the shapes more movement, helping to make them look less flat and more realistic. You can buy specialist foam trays for this purpose, but the recesses of an empty egg box or tray work equally well.

- A tiny dab of water can be used as a glue to stick shapes into place. For more strength, however, you will need to use an edible glue or royal icing.

- Gumpaste is a stronger alternative to sugarpaste. You can colour it in the same way but it can be rolled out much thinner and finer than sugarpaste – great for making rose petals – and it will dry out quicker too.

- Store any excess sugarpaste wrapped well in cling film (plastic wrap) and placed in a plastic bag to prevent it from drying out.

Making Sugarcraft Decorations

Cutters

For a crisp cut-out, after rolling out allow the sugarpaste to dry for a couple of minutes on the work surface. Dust your cutters gently with a sugar duster to prevent shapes from sticking. Press down the cutter and then move it in a circular motion to free it completely from the surrounding paste – this works away any little jagged flecks from the edge of the shape. If a shape doesn't release from the cutter straight away, it can be gently encouraged out using a soft clean paintbrush.

Plunger cutters

To use a plunger cutter, press down the cutter, keeping it in contact with the work surface and making sure the shape is cut out completely and is freed from the surrounding sugarpaste. Lift up the cutter with the shape still in place, then depress the plunger and release the shape onto your work surface.

Veiners

If you want to invest in a veiner, a large one is best, as it will add detail to all sizes of leaf. Gently dust both parts of the veiner with a sugar duster. Place your cut-out centrally on the base pieces. Position the top part carefully and gently press together to imprint the detail. Remove the top half and then gently release the veined leaf.

✎ TIP ✎

To create movement in a shape, lift out the cutter with the piece still in place, set the end onto your forefinger and gently depress the plunger – this will imprint the detail and shape the piece. Lift it away from your finger and press the plunger once again to release the shape.

How to Roll a Rose and Shape a Leaf

1. Take a small ball of sugarpaste (rolled fondant/ready-to-roll icing) about 3cm (1¼in) in diameter and shape by hand into a rough sausage shape 6cm (2½in) long.

2. In the palm of your hand, using the length of your forefinger, flatten one long edge.

3. Start to roll up the strip from one end to form the flower, keeping the roll fairly loose. Once the roll has started, hold it in your fingertips, shaping the 'petals' loosely away from each other.

4. Press the end into the flower to seal it together. Using a pair of scissors gently snip away the excess from the base of the rolled rose so that it will sit flat.

5. For the leaves, roll small balls of sugarpaste about 1cm (½in) in diameter and flatten with your finger. Pinch the end of the flattened ball to create the point of the leaf. Mark a central vein down the leaf with the back of a knife.

∽ TIP ∽

Lightly dust your hands with icing (confectioners') sugar before working directly with sugarpaste to prevent it from sticking.

HOW TO MAKE A PETAL ROSE

METHOD

1. Grease the work surface and your hands with a little vegetable fat to prevent the paste from sticking.

2. Make a small ball of paste and then taper one side to make a cone. This will form the base of the rose. Set it aside. Roll out some more paste very thinly to a thickness of 2–3mm ($\frac{1}{16}$–$\frac{1}{8}$in).

3. Cut out one small petal using the cutter. Transfer the petal to your foam pad. Take the large end of the ball tool and rub it over the very top edge of the petal. This thins the edge of the petal and creates a look of the natural movement of rose petals.

⤳ TIP ⤲

It is important to keep the ball tool moving across the edge of the petal, applying an even pressure, or the edge of the petal may tear.

⤳ TIP ⤲

You can make your own gumpaste by kneading in 1 teaspoon of Tylo powder (available from cake decorating suppliers) to 500g (1lb 2oz) of plain white sugarpaste. Wrap it well in cling film (plastic wrap) and allow it to develop overnight before using.

4. Add a dab of water with the paintbrush to the back of the petal. Wrap the petal around the cone to form the centre of the rose.

5. Cut out two more petals and again shape with the ball tool on the foam pad. Add a small dab of water at the base of each petal before sticking into place, wrapping it loosely around the previous petal. Encourage the edge of the petal to curl outwards.

⤳ TIP ⤳

Gumpaste roses can be made well in advance and once dried out stored in a non-airtight container, such as a cardboard box, for a considerable length of time until needed.

6. Continue to build up the rose adding further petals, increasing them in size as the flower gets bigger, to create an open flower shape. The average number of petals per rose is 10–12 for large flowers, 6–8 for medium and 3–4 for rosebuds. Place the rose in a recess of the egg box and allow to dry.

⤳ TIP ⤳

White roses can be lightly dusted with edible lustre dusts to add a hint of colour – simply apply using a large soft brush across the edges of the petals.

Lustre Dust

Edible lustre dusts are powdered colours used in dusting and decorating cakes. They come in all sorts of colours and add depth, sparkle and shading to sugarpaste (rolled fondant/ready-to-roll icing) pieces.

To dust

Apply to dry sugarpaste for a hint of colour. Using a soft brush with a light touch, tap off excess colour first, then build up the colour gradually to the required shade.

To paint

Using a paintbrush, mix a little of the dust with clear alcohol (such as vodka or gin) or rejuvenator fluid to form a paint and use immediately. Use to add vibrant detail to sugarpaste pieces. It dries quickly and won't affect the texture of the sugarpaste.

TIP

Dusts can be used to make a range of shades and mixed with rejuvenator fluid to form paints. A good basic set of dusts will allow you to create any colour you may need.

Royal Icing

Ready-mixed powdered royal icing is easy to use but make sure you only add water a very small amount at a time and then whisk the royal icing with an electric hand mixer until it thickens and forms medium-firm peaks. You can also make up your own royal icing by sifting 165g (5¾oz) icing (confectioners') sugar, then whisking together with 1 teaspoon Meri-White or egg-white powder and 15–25ml (1–1½ tablespoons) of water.

Colouring royal icing

Add a little gel paste colouring to the prepared white royal icing and beat well until smooth. Leave to stand for a couple of minutes to allow the colour to develop and then beat again before using.

How to Make a Sugar Duster

You will need a brand new all-purpose cleaning cloth, an elastic band, icing (confectioners') sugar and cornflour (cornstarch). Lay the cloth open on your work surface and place one generous tablespoonful each of sugar and cornflour in the centre. Gather the cloth around them and secure with an elastic band. This handy little duster can then be tapped on a surface for a very light dusting of sugar when making decorations and modelling.

Storing Sugarpaste

It is important to store any leftover sugarpaste correctly so that it will be fresh to use at a later date. Sugarpaste will quickly harden and become unusable if left in contact with the air. Wrap it well in cling film (plastic wrap), place inside a sealable plastic bag or airtight container and store at room temperature (not the fridge). As long as the container is airtight you can store it until the use-by date.

SUPPLIERS

UK

BAKING MAD
The Baking Mad Kitchen, Sugar Way
Peterborough PE2 9AY
Tel: 0800 880 5944
www.bakingmad.com
*Silverspoon, Allinson, Billington's,
and Nielsen-Massey extracts*

BAKERY BITS
1 Orchard Units, Duchy Road
Honiton, Devon EX14 1YD
Tel: 01404 565656
www.bakerybits.co.uk
Nibbed sugar and other baking equipment

CRAFTMILL
Unit 19C, Compstall Mill
Andrew Street, Compstall
Stockport SK6 5HN
Tel: 0161 484 5888
www.craftmill.co.uk
Polystyrene cones and craft supplies

STITCH CRAFT CREATE
Brunel House, Forde Close
Newton Abbot
Devon TQ12 4PU
Tel: 0844 880 5851
www.stitchcraftcreate.co.uk
*Books, tools and supplies for
baking and cake decorating*

WAITROSE
Doncastle Road, Bracknell
Berkshire RG12 8YA
www.waitrose.com
Freeze-dried mango and baking supplies

US

MICHAELS
8000 Bent Branch Dr.
Irving TX 75063
Tel: 1-800-642-4235
www.michaels.com
*Baking and cake decorating
equipment plus craft supplies*

A C MOORE ARTS & CRAFTS
Stores across the US
Tel: 1-888-226-667
www.acmoore.com
Baking, craft and cake decorating supplies

WILLIAMS-SONOMA
Locations across the US
Tel: 877-812-6235
www.williams-sonoma.com
*Bakeware, kitchenware and
kitchen electricals*

AUSTRALIA

KITCHEN WITCH
500 Hay Street
Subiaco WA 6008
Tel: 08 9380 4788
www.homeinwa.com.au
Bakeware and kitchen essentials

MYER
Stores across Australia
PO Box 869J
Melbourne VIC 3001
Phone: 1800 811 611
www.myer.com.au
Bakeware and other baking essentials

TARGET
Stores across Australia
Customer Relations, Reply Paid 41
Nth Geelong Vic 3215
Tel: 1800 814 788
www.target.com.au
Baking and kitchen equipment

ABOUT THE AUTHOR

RUTH CLEMENS is a passionate self-taught breadmaker, baker and cake decorator. She took part in the very first series of BBC2's *The Great British Bake Off* and to her own astonishment made it to the final. This is her fourth book to make it on to the shelves of bakers' kitchens far and wide. Ruth writes the hugely popular baking blog The Pink Whisk, featured in *The Independent*'s 50 Best Food Websites and packed full of recipes. To keep up to date with Ruth's most recent ventures, you can join the gang and ask any burning questions at facebook.com/ThePinkWhisk or on Twitter @thepinkwhisk – why not tempt her with your own éclair recipes? For lots more baking inspiration, tutorials and recipes visit www.thepinkwhisk.co.uk

ACKNOWLEDGMENTS

LOTS OF THANK YOUS ARE DUE! To my boys Ashley, Dylan and Finlay, and husband Damian, not so much for the taste testing – that's no hardship – but for putting up with me when I'm tearing my hair out because the recipes just aren't working, and for tolerating the telly ban while I'm writing. My huge thanks to Baking Mad, Silverspoon, Billington's and Allinson for a generous supply of ingredients that has seen me through from start to finish. Copious amounts of flour, chocolate and sugarpaste have made their way through my kitchen. As always, I'd also like to send a big virtual hug to the gang known as The Pink Whiskers, fellow kitchen tinkerers, a thoroughly lovely bunch who have completely given this stay-at-home baking-mad mummy a whole new career. And last but not least the team at David & Charles and the FW Media team for their support and super hard work to get this book together – Ame, James, Victoria, Katy, Emma and Nicky. Also to Jack for your beautiful photos (and for letting me torture you all day long with goodies you're not allowed to eat until we've finished. You must have willpower of steel).

INDEX

A DAVID & CHARLES BOOK
© F&W Media International, Ltd 2014

David & Charles is an imprint of F&W Media International, Ltd
Brunel House, Forde Close, Newton Abbot, TQ12 4PU, UK

F&W Media International, Ltd is a subsidiary of F+W Media, Inc
10151 Carver Road, Suite #200, Blue Ash, OH 45242, USA

Text and Designs © Ruth Clemens 2014
Layout and Photography © F&W Media International, Ltd 2014

First published in the UK and USA in 2014

A catalogue record for this book is available from the British Library.

ISBN-13: 978-1-4463-0387-0 paperback
ISBN-10: 1-4463-0387-X paperback

Printed in China by RR Donnelley for:
F&W Media International, Ltd
Brunel House, Forde Close, Newton Abbot, TQ12 4PU, UK

10 9 8 7 6 5 4 3 2 1

Acquisitions Editor: Ame Verso
Desk Editor: Emma Gardner
Project Editor: Nicky Gyopari
Senior Designer: Victoria Marks
Photographer: Jack Kirby
Production Manager: Beverley Richardson

F+W Media publishes high quality books on a wide range of subjects.
For more great book ideas visit: **www.stitchcraftcreate.co.uk**